ANTI-INFLAMMA[TORY]
DIET

cookbook

FOR BEGINNERS

COUNTLESS TASTY & EASY RECIPES TO REDUCE YOUR BODY INFLAMMATION, BALANCE HORMONES, AND HEAL THE IMMUNE SYSTEM. 6-WEEKS SMART MEAL PLAN

Lara Rush

Contents

ANTI-INFLAMMATORY DIET cookbook FOR BEGINNERS

BONUS INCLUDED

IBD- FOOD JOURNAL

Scroll to the end and scan the QR code to download your FREE PDF

INTRODUCTION

What is an Anti-Inflammatory Diet?

Inflammation is a normal immune response, but it can lead to various health problems when it becomes chronic. Arthritis, Crohn's disease, and asthma are the most common inflammatory diseases. While there is no cure for these conditions, treatments can help manage the symptoms. One of the most important things you can do is eat a healthy diet with anti-inflammatory foods. These foods help to reduce inflammation by keeping immune cells in check and reducing the production of inflammatory molecules. So, if you're looking to reduce inflammation, load up on these healthy foods.

An anti-inflammatory cookbook is a book of recipes designed to minimize inflammation in the body. Inflammation is a normal immune response that helps to protect the body from infection and disease. However, when inflammation becomes chronic, it can lead to various health problems, including heart disease, diabetes, and arthritis. The goal of an anti-inflammatory diet is to reduce chronic inflammation by avoiding foods that trigger the inflammatory response and by eating foods that help to reduce inflammation

How Does the Anti-Inflammatory Diet Work?

Inflammation is a response by the body to infection, irritation, or injury. The inflammatory process helps to remove harmful stimuli and to initiate the healing process. However, chronic inflammation can contribute to various health problems, including heart disease, arthritis, and diabetes. An anti-inflammatory diet can help to reduce the risk of these conditions by reducing the level of inflammation in the body.

The Anti-inflammatory diet is designed to help people suffering from chronic inflammation. The book contains recipes that use ingredients known to help reduce inflammation and information on which foods to avoid. The recipes in the book are categorized by type of food, so people can easily find the right recipe for their needs. In addition, the book includes tips on how to make the recipes more accessible for people with different dietary requirements. For example, many of the recipes can be made gluten-free or lactose-free. The Anti-inflammatory Cookbook is a valuable resource for anyone looking to reduce their inflammation levels.

Understanding the Food Choices.

Scientists have long known that inflammation is a key factor in many chronic diseases. From heart disease to arthritis, inflammatory conditions can lead to extensive damage and debilitating symptoms. In recent years, researchers have begun to explore the role of diet in inflammation, and they have found that certain foods can trigger or worsen inflammatory reactions. As a result, many people are turning to anti-inflammatory diets to protect their health.

While there is no one-size-fits-all approach to an anti-inflammatory diet, successful plans have some commonalities. Most notably, anti-inflammatory diets typically emphasize fruits, vegetables, and fish while limiting refined carbohydrates, red meat, and processed foods. This balance of nutrients helps to reduce inflammation throughout the body and promote overall health. In addition, many people who follow an anti-inflammatory diet also avoid dairy products, alcohol, and caffeine, as these substances can also contribute to inflammation.

The anti-inflammatory diet is a nutrient-rich eating plan that has been shown to offer numerous health benefits. Though there are many different versions of the diet, common food choices include fresh fruits and vegetables, whole grains, fish, olive oil, and nuts. These foods are rich in anti-inflammatory compounds like omega-3 fatty acids, antioxidants, and phytochemicals.

Benefits of the Anti-Inflammatory Diet.

Here are seven benefits of following an anti-inflammatory diet:

1. Fewer joint pains:
Inflammation can cause joint pain and stiffness, but by reducing inflammation through diet, you can experience significant relief.

2. Lower risk of heart disease:
High levels of inflammation have been linked to an increased risk of heart disease. By reducing inflammation, you can lower your risk.

3. Improved cognitive function:
A recent study found that people who followed an anti-inflammatory diet had better cognitive function than those who did not.

4. Reduced risk of cancer:
Some research has shown that inflammation can contribute to cancer development. By reducing inflammation, you may be able to lower your risk.

5. Better gut health:
An anti-inflammatory diet can help to reduce symptoms and improve gut health.

6. Improved skin health:
Inflammation can worsen skin conditions like eczema and psoriasis. An anti-inflammatory diet can help to improve skin health.

7. Greater overall well-being:
Reducing inflammation with diet can help you feel your best physically and mentally.

Benefits of the Anti-Inflammatory Cookbook

The anti-inflammatory cookbook is a great resource for people looking to improve their health and well-being. The recipes are based on scientific research and designed to help reduce inflammation in the body. Inflammation is a major contributor to many chronic diseases, such as heart disease, arthritis, and cancer. By reducing inflammation, we can reduce our risk of developing these conditions. The recipes in the cookbook are simple to follow and can be easily incorporated into a busy lifestyle. In addition, the cookbook includes tips on how to shop for anti-inflammatory ingredients and how to prepare meals that are both nutritious and delicious. With its emphasis on healthy eating, an anti-inflammatory cookbook is an essential tool for anyone looking to improve their health. However, chronic inflammation can lead to various health problems like heart disease, arthritis, and diabetes. Many foods contribute to inflammation, but many anti-inflammatory foods can also help reduce it. Some of the top benefits of following an anti-inflammatory cookbook include:

1. Reducing the risk of chronic diseases:
By following an anti-inflammatory diet, you can help to reduce your risk of developing these conditions.

2. Improving gut health:
Following an anti-inflammatory diet can help to improve gut health by reducing inflammation.

3. Promoting weight loss:
An anti-inflammatory diet can help you lose weight and keep it off.

4. Enhancing brain health:
An anti-inflammatory diet can help to improve brain function and prevent age-related cognitive degeneration.

5. Improving skin health:
You can help to improve your skin health by adopting an anti-inflammatory diet.

6. Reducing pain:
An anti-inflammatory diet can help relieve pain associated with arthritis and fibromyalgia.

7. Regulating hormonal levels:
by following an anti-inflammatory diet may help to regulate hormones and alleviate symptoms of conditions like PCOS and endometriosis.

8. Lowering stress levels:
Inflammatory foods have been linked to increased stress levels, so an anti-inflammatory diet may help lower stress levels and promote relaxation.

Banned Foods
The anti-inflammatory diet is a way of eating that emphasizes whole, unprocessed foods and minimizes foods that can contribute to inflammation. Proponents of the diet claim that it can help improve various health conditions, from joint pain to asthma. Foods banned in the anti-inflammatory diet include processed meats, dairy, processed cheeses, refined carbohydrates, sugary drinks, fried foods, etc.
These foods all contribute to inflammation in the body, so it is best to avoid them if you are trying to reduce inflammation.

Foods Allowed

The anti-inflammatory diet is based on the theory that chronic inflammation is a major contributor to many diseases. The goal of the diet is to reduce inflammation by avoiding inflammatory foods and eating anti-inflammatory foods. Anti-inflammatory foods include fruits, vegetables, whole grains, fish, lean protein, and healthy fats. Spices like cinnamon, cumin and turmeric are also important in an anti-inflammatory diet.

The anti-inflammatory diet is a healing diet based on eating whole, unprocessed foods rich in nutrients. The goal of the diet is to reduce inflammation in the body, which has been linked to various health problems, including heart disease, arthritis, and cancer. In addition to eating an anti-inflammatory diet, it is also important to get regular exercise and avoid smoking and excessive alcohol consumption. These simple lifestyle changes can dramatically reduce your risk of chronic diseases.

FAQ'S

Anti-Inflammatory Diet and Parkinson's
Recent studies have shown that an anti-inflammatory diet may help to protect against Parkinson's disease. Parkinson's is a degenerative neurological disorder that affects movement and often leads to tremors, stiffness, and balance problems. While there is no cure for Parkinson's, researchers believe that an anti-inflammatory diet may help to prevent or delay the onset of the disease. The diet includes fish, green leafy vegetables, olive oil, nuts, and berries. These foods are rich in antioxidants and omega-3 fatty acids, which have anti-inflammatory properties.

Anti-Inflammatory Diet and Depression
Depression is a serious mental health condition that can profoundly impact every aspect of a person's life. While medication and therapy are often effective treatments, there is growing evidence that diet can play an important role in managing depression. An anti-inflammatory diet focuses on eating foods that help reduce inflammation. Inflammation has been linked to depression, so by reducing inflammation and thinking, we can also help to reduce symptoms of depression. Some of the best anti-inflammatory foods include omega-3 fatty acids, turmeric, ginger, and green leafy vegetables. While more research is needed, an anti-inflammatory diet is a promising approach for managing depression.

Anti-Inflammatory Diet and Cancer Prevention
The anti-inflammatory diet is gaining popularity in preventing chronic diseases such as cancer. While there is still much to learn about the connection between inflammation and cancer, there is evidence that a diet rich in anti-inflammatory foods can help to reduce the risk of developing cancer. Some of the best anti-inflammatory foods include omega-3 fatty acids, antioxidants, and phytochemicals. Salmon, dark leafy greens, berries, and tomatoes are all excellent sources of these nutrients. In addition to eating more anti-inflammatory foods, people can also reduce their cancer risk by exercising regularly, maintaining a healthy weight, and avoiding tobacco use.

Can Anti-Inflammatory Diet Help in Weight Loss?

There is growing evidence that inflammation plays a role in obesity and weight gain. Chronic inflammation can lead to insulin resistance, which in turn can lead to weight gain. Inflammation can also increase the number of fat cells in the body and make it harder to lose weight.

Many foods can contribute to inflammation, including processed foods, refined sugars, and omega-6 fatty acids. However, several foods have anti-inflammatory properties. These include omega-3 fatty acids, ginger, turmeric, and green tea. An anti-inflammatory diet is a promising option for those looking to manage their weight healthily.

Do Anti-Inflammatory Diet Work?

A growing body of evidence suggests that inflammation may be the root cause of many chronic diseases, from heart disease and arthritis to diabetes and cancer. As a result, many people are turning to anti-inflammatory diets to improve their health. But do these diets work?

There is no one-size-fits-all answer to this question, as each person's inflammatory response is unique. However, several studies have shown that anti-inflammatory diets can help to reduce the risk of chronic disease. For example, a recent study found that a diet rich in anti-inflammatory foods was associated with a lower risk of heart disease.

So, while there is no guarantee that an anti-inflammatory diet will work for everyone, there is evidence that it can benefit many people. If you are interested in trying an anti-inflammatory diet, talk to your doctor or a registered dietitian to get started.

How Does Anti-Inflammatory Diet Work?

Dietary inflammation contributes to chronic diseases such as heart disease, cancer, and diabetes. The anti-inflammatory diet is a way of eating that minimizes the dietary inflammatory response. The goal of the diet is to reduce chronic inflammation throughout the body. Eating unprocessed foods is less likely to trigger an inflammatory response than processed foods. Second, the diet emphasizes healthy fats, which have anti-inflammatory properties. Finally, the diet includes a variety of antioxidants and phytonutrients, which help to reduce inflammation throughout the body. Following an anti-inflammatory diet can minimize your risk of chronic disease and promote overall health and wellness.

What Foods are Good for an Anti-Inflammatory Diet?

Several foods are thought to be good for an anti-inflammatory diet. These include omega-3 fatty acids in fish, fruits, vegetables and whole grains. Some studies have also suggested that certain spices, such as turmeric, ginger, and garlic, may also be beneficial. While no one magic food or nutrient will completely protect against inflammation, incorporating these foods into your diet may help to reduce your risk.

Why is Anti-Anti-Inflammatory Diet Important?

Chronic inflammation has been linked to various health problems, including heart disease, arthritis, diabetes, and even cancer. While there are many potential causes of chronic inflammation, diet is thought to be one of the most important factors. A diet rich in processed foods, refined sugars, and unhealthy fats can promote inflammation throughout the body. On the other hand, a diet that includes plenty of fresh fruits and vegetables, whole grains, and healthy fats can help to reduce inflammation. In particular, omega-3 fatty acids have been shown to have anti-inflammatory effects. For people struggling with chronic inflammation, an anti-inflammatory diet may effectively reduce symptoms and improve overall health.

How Anti-Inflammatory Diet is Good for You?

An anti-inflammatory diet is a way of eating to reduce inflammation throughout the body. While inflammation is a normal response by the immune system to protect against injury and infection, chronic inflammation can lead to several serious health problems, including heart disease, diabetes, and arthritis. The anti-inflammatory diet focuses on eating foods that help to reduce inflammation while avoiding inflammatory foods. Some of the best anti-inflammatory foods include omega-3-rich fish, fruits and vegetables, whole grains, nuts, and seeds. In contrast, some of the worst foods for inflammation are processed meats, sugar, trans fats, and refined carbs. By following an anti-inflammatory diet, you can help to reduce your risk of developing chronic diseases.

Anti-Inflammatory Diet and Exercise

A growing body of evidence suggests that inflammation may be at the root of many chronic diseases. These include heart disease, cancer, Alzheimer's disease, and diabetes. As a result, many people are looking for ways to reduce inflammation through diet and exercise. Exercise helps reduce inflammation by promoting blood flow and helping the body eliminate toxins. Furthermore, it has been shown to boost the immune system, which can help to fight off inflammatory diseases.

Following an anti-inflammatory diet and exercise routine can help reduce your risk of developing chronic diseases. In addition, you may also experience other benefits such as weight loss, improved energy levels, and better sleep.

BREAKFAST

RECIPES

Raspberry Smoothie Bowl

Prep Time: 10 mins.| Serves: 2

1 C. frozen raspberries
¼ C. unflavored protein powder
¼ C. MCT oil
2 tbsp. chia seeds
1 tsp. organic vanilla extract
4 drops liquid stevia
1½ C. unsweetened almond milk

Add frozen raspberries and remaining ingredients in a high-power blender and pulse until smooth.
Transfer into 3 serving bowls and serve with your favorite topping.

Per Serving:
Calories: 258| Fat: 22.g| Carbs: 9g| Fiber: 4.9g| Protein: 11.1g

Fruity Chia Bowl

Prep Time: 15 mins.| Serves: 2

2 C. frozen cherries, pitted
4 dates, pitted and chopped roughly1 large apple, peeled, cored and chopped
1 C. fresh cherries, pitted
2 tbsp. chia seeds

In a high-power blender, add frozen cherries and dates and pulse until smooth.
In a large-sized bowl, mix together apples, fresh cherries and chia seeds.
Add the cherry sauce and stir to combine.
Cover and refrigerate to chill overnight before serving.

Per Serving:
Calories: 183| Fat: 6g| Carbs: 32.7g| Fiber: 6g| Protein: 4.5g

Spiced Oatmeal

Prep Time: 10 mins.| Cook Time: 3 mins.| Serves: 2

2/3 C. unsweetened coconut milk
½ C. gluten-free quick-cooking oats
1 organic egg white
½ tsp. ground turmeric
½ tsp. ground cinnamon
¼ tsp. ground ginger

In a microwave-safe bowl, blend together milk and oats and microwave on a High setting for about 1 minute.
Remove from the microwave and stir in the egg white until well blended.
Add in the spices and stir until well blended.
Microwave on a High setting for about 2 minutes, stirring after every 20 seconds.
Serve warm with your favorite topping.

Per Serving:
Calories: 129| Fat: 3.3g| Carbs: 17.9g|
Fiber: 3g| Protein: 5.7g

Quinoa & Pumpkin Porridge

Prep Time: 10 mins.| Cook Time: 17 mins.| Serves: 6

3½ C. filtered water
1¾ C. quinoa, soaked for 15 minutes and rinsed
16 oz. unsweetened coconut milk
1¾ C. sugar-free pumpkin puree
2 tsp. ground cinnamon
1 tsp. ground ginger
Pinch of ground cloves
Pinch of ground nutmeg
Salt, as required
3 tbsp. extra-virgin coconut oil
4-6 drops liquid stevia
1 tsp. organic vanilla extract

In a saucepan, add the water and quinoa over high heat.
Cover the pan and bring to a boil.
Reduce the heat to low and simmer for about 12 minutes or until all the liquid is absorbed.
Add the remaining ingredients and stir until well combined.
Immediately remove from the heat and serve warm.

Per Serving:
Calories: 285|
Fat: 11.3g| Carbs: 39.2g| Fiber: 6.3g| Protein: 7.9g

ANTI-INFLAMMATORY DIET cookbook FOR BEGINNERS

Banana Pancakes

Prep Time: 10 mins.| Cook Time: 10 mins.| Serves: 2

¼ C. arrowroot flour
¼ C. gluten-free rolled oats
½ tsp. organic baking powder
¼ tsp. baking soda
1/8 tsp. ground cinnamon
¼ C. unsweetened almond milk
2 organic egg whites
2 tsp. coconut oil, softened and divided
½ of banana, peeled and mashed
1/8 tsp. organic vanilla extract

Place the oats, flour, baking powder, baking soda and cinnamon in a large-sized bowl and mix well.
In another bowl, add the milk, egg whites, 1 tsp. of coconut oil, banana and vanilla extract and beat until well combined.
Add egg mixture into flour mixture and mix until well combined.
Place the oats, flour, baking powder, baking soda and cinnamon in a large-sized bowl and mix well.
In another bowl, add the milk, egg whites, 1 tsp. of coconut oil, banana and vanilla extract and beat until well combined.
Add the flour mixture into milk mixture and mix until well combined.
Grease a large-sized frying pan with remaining coconut oil and heat over low heat.
Add half of the mixture and cook for about 1-2 minutes per side.
Repeat with the remaining mixture.
Serve warm

Per Serving:
Calories: 145|
Fat: 6.1g| Carbs: 18g| Fiber: 2.5g|
Protein: 6.5g

Spinach & Egg Scramble

Prep Time: 10 mins.| Cook Time: 6 mins.| Serves:2

4 organic eggs
2 tbsp. coconut oil
2 C. fresh spinach, chopped
1 tsp. garlic powder
¼ tsp. ground turmeric
1/3 tsp. red pepper flakes, crushed
Salt and ground black pepper, as required

In a bowl, add the eggs and whisk well.
In a wok, melt the coconut oil over medium heat and cook spinach for about 2 minutes.
Add the eggs and remaining ingredients and cook for about 3-4 minutes or until desired doneness, stirring frequently.
Serve hot.

Per Serving:
Calories: 257|
Fat: 22.6g| Carbs: 3.1g| Fiber: 0.9g|
Protein: 12.2g

Turmeric Bread

Prep Time: 10 mins.| Cook Time: 20 mins.| Serves: 8

Olive oil cooking spray
½ C. plus 1 tbsp. almond flour
1 tsp. baking soda
1¼ tsp. ground turmeric
Salt, as required
2 large organic eggs
2 organic egg whites
1 C. almond butter
1 tbsp. water
1 tbsp. apple cider vinegar

Preheat your oven to 350 ºF.
Grease a loaf pan with cooking spray.
In a large-sized pan, blend together flour, baking soda, turmeric and salt.
In another bowl, add eggs, egg whites and almond butter and beat until smooth.
Gradually add water and beat until well blended.
Add flour mixture and mix until well blended.
Stir in apple cider vinegar.
Place the mixture into the prepared loaf pan evenly.
Bake for approximately 20 minutes or until a wooden skewer inserted in the center comes out clean.
. Carefully remove the loaf from pan and place onto the wire rack to cool fully before slicing.
. Cut the bread loaf into desired-sized slices and serve.

Per Serving:
Calories: 145|
Fat: 8.8g|
Carbs: 10.2g|
Fiber: 1.9g|
Protein: 4.4g

Veggie Frittata

Prep Time: 15 mins.| Cook Time: 17 mins.| Serves: 3

1-2 tbsp. coconut oil
½-1 tsp. ground turmeric
1 small bell pepper, seeded and chopped
1 C. fresh kale leaves, tough ribs removed and chopped
¼ C. scallion greens, chopped
6 organic eggs
Salt, as required

In a cast-iron wok, melt the coconut oil over medium-low heat.
Sprinkle turmeric in the oil and immediately stir in bell pepper, kale and scallion greens.
Cook for about 2 minutes, stirring continuously.
Meanwhile, in a bowl, add eggs and salt and beat well.
Now adjust the heat to low.
Add beaten eggs in the wok over bell pepper mixture evenly.
Cover and cook for about 10-15 minutes.
Remove the wok of frittata from heat and set aside for about 5 minutes before serving.

Per Serving:
Calories: 191|
Fat: 13.5g| Carbs: 6.4g| Fiber: 1g|
Protein: 12.4g

ANTI-INFLAMMATORY DIET cookbook FOR BEGINNERS

Blueberry Muffins

Prep Time: 10 mins.| Cook Time: 24 mins.| Serves: 12

Olive oil cooking spray
2½ C. almond flour
1 tbsp. coconut flour
½ tsp. baking soda
3 tbsp. ground cinnamon, divided
Salt, as required
2 organic eggs
¼ C. unsweetened coconut milk
¼ C. coconut oil
¼ C. organic honey
1 tbsp. organic vanilla extract
1 C. fresh blueberries

Preheat your oven to 350 ºF.
Grease a 12 cups standard-sized muffin tin with cooking spray.
In a bowl, blend together both flours, baking soda, 2 tbsp. of cinnamon and salt.
In another bowl, add eggs, milk, oil, honey and vanilla extract and beat until well blended.
In the bowl of flour mixture, add the egg mixture and mix until well blended.
Fold in the blueberries.
Place the mixture into the prepared muffin cups. evenly and sprinkle each with cinnamon evenly.
Bake for approximately 22-25 minutes or until a wooden skewer inserted in the center comes out clean.
Remove the muffin tin from oven and place onto a wire rack to cool for about 10 minutes.
. Carefully invert the muffins onto the wire rack to cool completely before serving.

Per Serving:
Calories: 252| Fat: 19.2g| Carbs: 14.3g| Fiber: 4.2g| Protein: 1.4g

Apple Omelet

Prep Time: 10 mins.| Cook Time: 10 mins.| Serves: 1

2 large organic eggs
1/8 tsp. organic vanilla extract
Pinch of salt
2 tsp. coconut oil, divided
½ of a large-sized apple, cored and thinly sliced
¼ tsp. ground cinnamon
1/8 tsp. ground ginger
1/8 tsp. ground nutmeg

In a bowl, add the eggs, vanilla extract and salt and beat until fluffy.
Set aside.
In a non-stick frying pan, melt 1 tsp. of coconut oil over medium-low heat.
Sprinkle the apple slices with spices evenly and place in the pan in a single layer.
Cook for about 4-5 minutes, flipping once halfway through.
Add the remaining oil in the wok.
Add the egg mixture over apple slices evenly.
Tilt the pan to spread the egg mixture evenly.
Cook for about 3-4 minutes.
. Transfer the omelet onto a plate and serve.

Per Serving:
Calories: 284| Fat: 19.1g| Carbs: 16g| Fiber: 3.1g| Protein: 12.9g

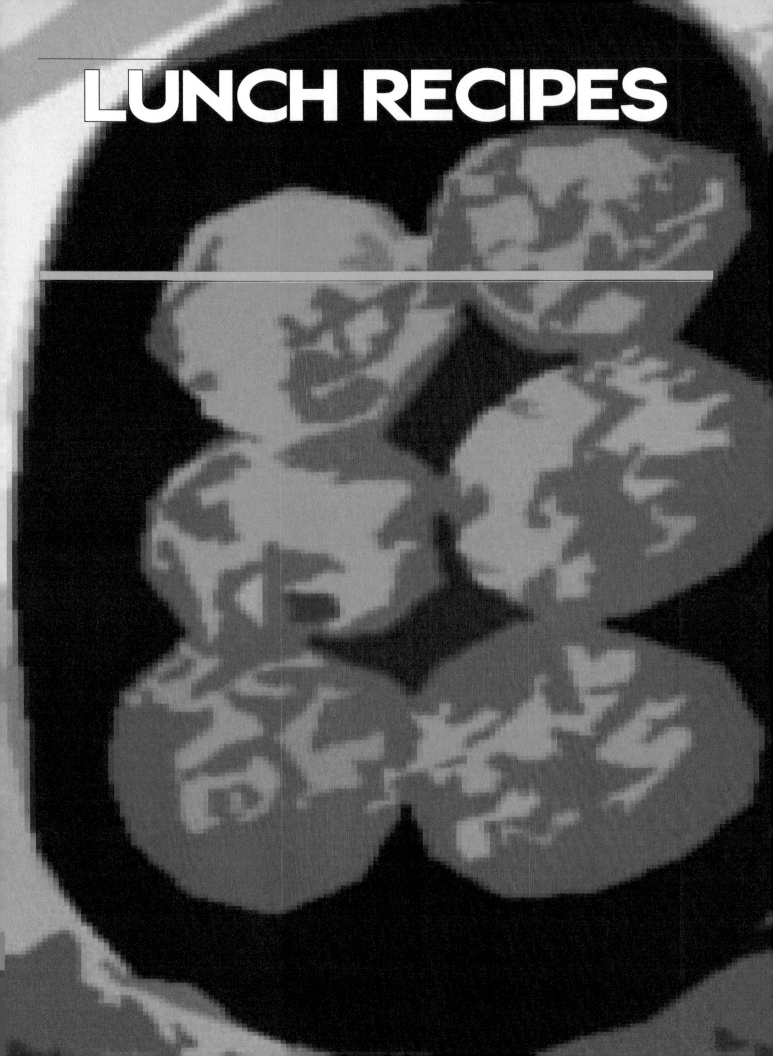

LUNCH RECIPES

Egg Drop Soup

Prep Time: 10 mins.| Cook Time: 20 mins.| Serves: 6

1 tbsp. olive oil
½ tbsp. garlic, minced
½ tbsp. fresh ginger, minced
6 C. homemade chicken broth, divided
2 organic eggs
1 tbsp. arrowroot flour
1/3 C. fresh lemon juice
Salt and ground white pepper, as required
¼ C. scallion (green part), chopped

In a large-sized soup pan, heat the oil over medium-high heat and sauté garlic and ginger for about 1 minute.
Add 5½ C. of broth and bring to a boil over high heat.
Reduce the heat to medium and simmer for about 5 minutes.
Meanwhile, in a bowl, add eggs, arrowroot four, lemon juice, salt, white pepper and remaining broth and beat until well combined.
Slowly add egg mixture in the pan, stirring continuously.
Simmer for about 5-6 minutes or until desired thickness of soup, stirring continuously
Serve hot with the garnishing of scallion greens.

Per Serving:
Calories: 64| Fat: 3.9g| Carbs: 2.4g| Fiber: 0.3g| Protein: 4.2g

Mushroom Soup

Prep Time: 15 mins.| Cook Time: 20 mins.| Serves: 3

3 C. homemade vegetable broth
1 C. fresh button mushrooms, slice
1 C. cherry tomatoes, chopped
½ of white onion, sliced
3 slices lemongrass
3 pieces fresh ginger
5 fresh kaffir lime leaves
2 Serrano peppers, seeded and mashed
2 tbsp. fresh lime juice
2 tbsp. coconut aminos
2 tbsp. fresh cilantro, chopped

In a large-sized pan, add broth over medium-high heat and bring to a boil.
Add the remaining ingredients except for cilantro over medium heat and again bring to a gentle simmer.
Simmer for about 15 minutes.
Remove the soup pan from heat and discard lemongrass, ginger and lime leaves.
Serve hot with the garnishing of cilantro.

Per Serving:
Calories: 56| Fat: 0.3g| Carbs: 9.4g| Fiber: 1.7g| Protein: 3.7g

Zucchini Lettuce Wraps

Prep Time: 15 mins.| Cook Time: 15 mins.| Serves: 4

1 tbsp. olive oil
1 tsp. cumin seeds
1 small yellow onion, thinly sliced
4 C. zucchini, grated
½ tsp. red pepper flakes, crushed
Salt and ground black pepper, as required
8 large lettuce leaves, rinsed and pat dried
2 tbsp. fresh chives, minced finely

In a medium-sized wok, heat the oil over medium-high heat and sauté the cumin seeds for about 1 minute.
Add the onion and sauté for about 4-6 minutes.
Add the zucchini and cook for about 5-7 minutes or until done completely, stirring occasionally.
Stir in the red pepper flakes, salt and black pepper and remove from the heat.
Arrange the lettuce leaves onto a smooth surface.
Divide the zucchini mixture onto each lettuce leaf evenly.
Top with the chives and serve immediately.

Per Serving:
Calories: 60| Fat: 3.9g| Carbs: 6.2g| Fiber: 1.8g| Protein: 1.9g

Stuffed Bell Peppers

Prep Time: 15 mins.| Cook Time: 24 mins.| Serves: 4

Per Serving:
Calories: 296| Fat: 5.5g| Carbs: 55.3g| Fiber: 9.3g| Protein: 10.2g

Olive oil cooking spray
2 C. cooked brown rice
1 tbsp. coconut oil
1 small can corn
15 oz. canned kidney beans, rinsed and drained
2 tsp. ground cumin
1 tsp. ground turmeric
1 tsp. garlic powder
1 tsp. red chili powder
Salt and ground black pepper, as required
2 tbsp. fresh parsley, chopped
4 large bell peppers, tops and seeds removed

Preheat your oven to 375 ºF.
Grease a large-sized baking sheet with cooking spray.
In a large-sized non-stick wok, melt coconut oil over medium heat and cook the rice, corns, beans and spices for about 2-3 minutes, stirring frequently.
Stir in parsley and remove from heat.
Stuff the bell peppers with rice mixture evenly.
Arrange the bell peppers onto the prepared baking sheet.
Bake for approximately 15-20 minutes.
Serve warm.

ANTI-INFLAMMATORY DIET cookbook FOR BEGINNERS

Stuffed Zucchini

Prep Time: 20 mins.| Cook Time: 30 mins.| Serves: 8

4 large zucchinis, halved lengthwise
Salt, as required
1½ baking potatoes, peeled and cubed
4 tsp. olive oil
2½ C. onion, chopped
1 Serrano pepper, mined
2 garlic cloves, minced
1½ tbsp. fresh ginger root, minced
2 tbsp. chickpea flour
1 tsp. ground coriander
¼ tsp. ground cumin
¼ tsp. ground turmeric
Freshly ground black pepper, as required
1½ C. frozen green peas, thawed
2 tbsp. fresh cilantro, chopped

Per Serving: Calories: 169| Fat: 3.2g| Carbs: 32.1g| Fiber: 7.6g| Protein: 6.5g

Preheat your oven to 375 ºF.
With a scooper, scoop out the pulp from zucchini halves, leaving about ¼-inch thick shell.
In a shallow roasting pan, arrange the zucchini halves, cut side up.
Sprinkle the zucchini halves with a little salt.
In a pan of boiling water, cook the potatoes for about 2 minutes. Drain well and set aside.
In a large-sized non-stick wok, heat oil over medium-high heat and sauté onion, Serrano, garlic and ginger for about 3 minutes. Now adjust the heat to medium-low.
Stir in chickpea flour and spices and cook for about 5 minutes.
. Sir in cooked potato, green peas and cilantro and remove from heat.
. With a paper towel, pat dry the zucchini halves.
. Stuff the zucchini halves with the veggie mixture evenly,
. Cover the baking dish and bake for approximately 20 minutes.
. Serve warm.

Scallops In Yogurt Sauce

Prep Time: 15 mins.| Cook Time: 13 mins.| Serves: 4

2 tbsp. coconut milk
½ C. shallot, minced
¼ C. tomato paste
2 tsp. fresh ginger root paste
2 tsp. garlic paste
½ tsp. garam masala powder
¼ tsp. ground cinnamon
¼ tsp. ground cumin
Pinch of cayenne pepper
Salt, as required
1 lb. sea scallops
8 oz. plain Greek yogurt, whipped

In a large-sized wok, melt coconut oil over medium-high heat and sauté shallots for about 2-3 minutes.
Add remaining ingredients except for scallops, yogurt and cilantro and cook for about 3-5 minutes.
Stir in scallops and yogurt and cook for about 5 minutes.
Serve hot.

Per Serving: Calories: 191| Fat: 3.5g| Carbs: 14.9g| Fiber: 1.1g| Protein: 23.9g

Shrimp In Lemon Sauce

Prep Time: 15 mins.| Cook Time: 10 mins.| Serves: 6

1 small onion, finely chopped
1 tbsp. fresh ginger root, minced
2 garlic cloves, minced
1 tbsp. fresh lemon zest, finely grated
1 fresh green chili pepper, seeded and minced
1 tsp. ground turmeric
½ C. olive oil
½ C. fresh lemon juice
20-24 raw shrimp, peeled and deveined
1 tbsp. coconut oil

In a bowl, blend together all ingredients except for shrimp and coconut oil.
Add shrimp and coat with marinade generously.
Cover and refrigerate to marinate overnight.
Remove the shrimp from bowl, reserving marinade.
In a large-sized non-stick wok, melt coconut oil over medium-high heat and stir fry for about 3-4 minutes.
Add reserved marinade and cook until boiling, tossing occasionally.
Cook for about 1-2 minutes.
Serve hot.

Per Serving:
Calories: 268| Fat: 20.6g| Carbs: 4.2g| Fiber: 0.6g| Protein: 17.2g

Three Veggie Medley

Prep Time: 15 mins.| Cook Time: 12 mins.| Serves: 3

For Mushroom Marinade
2 tsp. fresh ginger, minced
2 garlic cloves, minced
3-4 tbsp. organic honey
3-4 tbsp. coconut aminos
3 tbsp. fresh lime juice
1 tbsp. sesame oil
1 tbsp. water
2 Portobello mushrooms, sliced into thin strips
For Vegetables
1 tbsp. sesame seeds
1 C. broccolini, chopped
1 red bell pepper, seeded and thinly sliced
1 C. scallion, chopped

For marinade: in a large-sized bowl, add all ingredients except for mushrooms and mix until well combined.
Add mushrooms and coat with marinade generously.
Set aside for about 10-12 minutes.
In a large-sized non-stick wok, heat sesame oil over medium heat.
Remove the mushrooms from marinade and add in the wok in 2 batches and sauté for about 2-4 minutes per side.
Transfer the mushrooms in a bowl and cover with a piece of foil to keep warm.
In the same wok, add broccolini and bell pepper and sauté for about 2-3 minutes.
Add scallion and any remaining marinade from the bowl and sauté for about 1 minute.
Remove from heat and immediately mix with mushrooms.
. Serve immediately.

Per Serving:
Calories: 189| Fat: 6.4g| Carbs: 31.8g| Fiber: 3.3g| Protein: 4.4g

Potato Curry

Prep Time: 15 mins.| Cook Time: 12½ mins.| Serves: 3

1½ C. potato, finely chopped
2 tbsp. sweet corn kernels
1 C. plus 5 tbsp. water, divided
1 tbsp. olive oil
¼ C. onion, chopped
1 tbsp. celery chopped
2 C. unsweetened coconut milk
2 tbsp. arrowroot flour
Salt and ground black pepper, as required
2 tbsp. fresh cilantro, chopped

Place the potato, corn and water in a microwave-safe shallow dish and mix well.
Microwave on a High setting for about 6 minutes.
Remove from the microwave and set aside.
Place the oil in a microwave-safe bowl and microwave on a High setting for about 10-15 seconds.
In the bowl, add the onion and celery and microwave on a High setting for about 1 minute, stirring once halfway through.
Remove the bowl from microwave and stir in the cooked potato mixture and remaining water.
Microwave on a High setting for about 1 minute.
Meanwhile, place the milk and flour in a bowl and mix well.
Remove the bowl from the microwave and stir in the flour mixture until well combined.
Microwave on a High setting for about 4 minutes, stirring after every 1½ minutes.
Remove the bowl from microwave and stir in the salt and black pepper.
Serve hot with the garnishing of cilantro.

Per Serving: Calories: 135| Fat: 8.1g| Carbs: 14.2g| Fiber: 1.3g| Protein: 2g

Spiced Ground Beef

Prep Time: 10 mins.| Cook Time: 22 mins.| Serves: 5

2 tbsp. coconut oil
2 whole cloves
2 whole cardamoms
1 (2-inch) piece cinnamon stick
2 bay leaves
1 tsp. cumin seeds
2 onions, chopped
Salt, as required
½ tbsp. garlic paste
½ tbsp. fresh ginger paste
1 lb. grass-fed lean ground beef
1 tsp. ground cumin
1½ tsp. red chili powder
1/8 tsp. ground turmeric
Ground black pepper, as required
1 C. unsweetened coconut milk
¼ C. water
¼ C. fresh cilantro, chopped

In a large-sized pan, heat oil over medium heat and sauté cloves, cardamoms, cinnamon stick, bay leaves and cumin seeds for about 20-30 seconds.
Add onion and 2 pinches of salt and sauté for about 3-4 minutes.
Add garlic-ginger paste and sauté for about 2 minutes.
Add beef and cook for about 4-5 minutes, breaking into pieces with the spoon.
Cover and cook for about 5 minutes.
Stir in spices and cook for about 2-2½ minutes, stirring continuously.
Stir in coconut milk and water and cook for about 7-8 minutes.
Season with salt and remove from heat.
Serve hot with the garnishing of cilantro.

Per Serving: Calories: 352| Fat: 22.8g| Carbs: 8.1g| Fiber: 2.4g| Protein: 29.4g

DINNER RECIPES

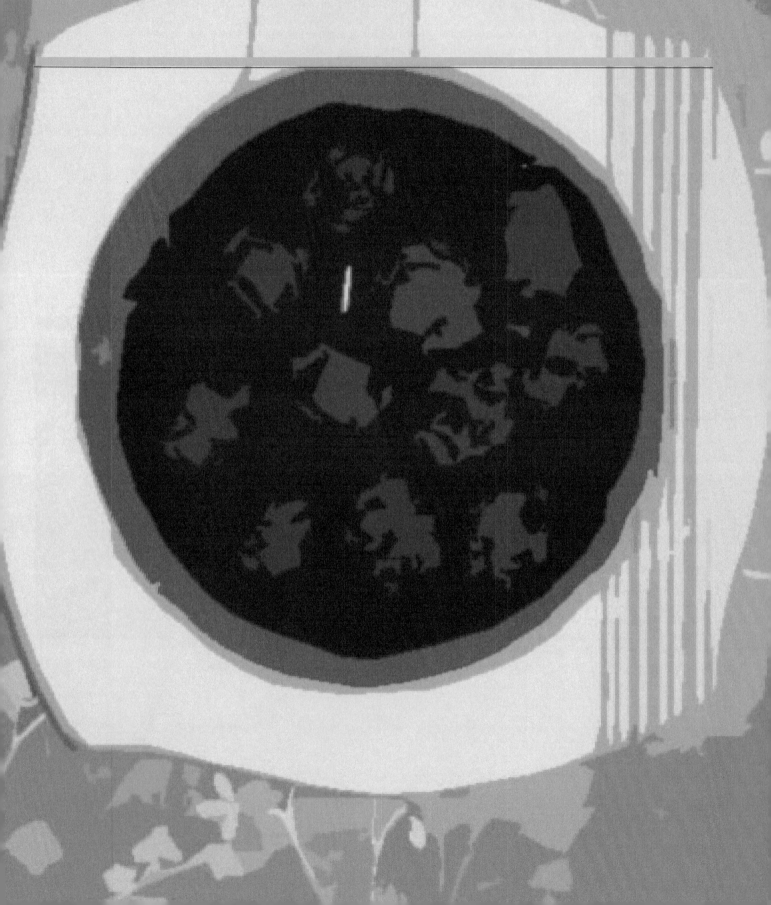

Beef & Mushroom Soup

Prep Time: 15 mins.| Cook Time: 20 mins.| Serves: 8

8 C. homemade chicken broth
2-3 C. broccoli, chopped
8 oz. fresh mushrooms, sliced
1 bunch scallion, chopped (reserve dark green part for garnishing)
1 (1-inch) piece fresh ginger root, minced
4 garlic cloves, minced
1½ lb. cooked beef meat, thinly sliced
½ tsp. red pepper flakes, crushed
3 tbsp. coconut aminos

In a soup pan, add broth and bring to a rolling boil.
Stir in broccoli pieces and cook for about 1-2 minutes.
Stir in mushroom, scallions, ginger and garlic and simmer for about 7-8 minutes.
Stir in beef, red pepper flakes and coconut aminos and adjust the heat to low.
Simmer for about 3-5 minutes.
Serve hot with the garnishing of reserved green part of scallion.

Per Serving:
Calories: 222| Fat: 6.9g| Carbs: 5.9g| Fiber: 1.2g| Protein: 32.5g

Beans & Lentil Soup

Prep Time: 15 mins.| Cook Time: 40 mins.| Serves: 6

1 tbsp. olive oil
2 garlic cloves, minced
2 carrots, peeled and finely chopped
1 yellow onion, finely chopped
1 C. dried lentils
1 (15-oz.) can diced tomatoes
1 (15½-oz.) can black beans, drained and rinsed
¾-1 tsp. chili powder
½ tsp. ground cumin
½ tsp. red pepper flakes, crushed
Salt and ground black pepper, as required
4 C. homemade vegetable broth

In a large-sized pan, heat the oil over medium heat and sauté garlic for bout 1 minute.
Add the carrots and onion and sauté for about 5 minutes.
Stir in the remaining ingredients and bring to a rolling boil.
Adjust the heat to low and simmer, covered for about 25-30 minutes, stirring occasionally.
Serve hot.

Per Serving:
Calories: 285| Fat: 4.3g| Carbs: 44g| Fiber: 18g| Protein: 18.9g

Chicken & Spinach Stew

Prep Time: 15 mins.| Cook Time: 35 mins.| Serves: 5

2 tbsp. extra-virgin olive oil
1 yellow onion, chopped
1 tbsp. garlic, minced
1 tbsp. fresh ginger root, minced
1 tsp. ground turmeric
1 tsp. ground cumin
1 tsp. ground coriander
1 tsp. paprika
4 (4-oz.) boneless, skinless chicken thighs, cut into 1-inch pieces
4 tomatoes, chopped
14 oz. unsweetened coconut milk
Salt and ground black pepper, as required
6 C. fresh spinach, chopped
2 tbsp. fresh lemon juice

Heat oil in a large-sized heavy-bottomed pan over medium heat and sauté the onion for about 3-4 minutes.
Add the ginger, garlic, and spices and sauté for about 1 minute.
Add the chicken and cook for about 4-5 minutes.
Add the tomatoes, coconut milk, salt, and black pepper, and bring to a gentle simmer.
Now, adjust the heat to low and simmer, covered for about 10-15 minutes.
Stir in the spinach and cook for about 4-5 minutes.
Add in lemon juice and remove from heat.
Serve hot.

Per Serving:
Calories: 279| Fat: 14.3g| Carbs: 9.44g| Fiber: 3.1g| Protein: 28.7g

---

Turkey & Chickpeas Chili

Prep Time: 15 mins.| Cook Time: 45 mins.| Serves: 6

Per Serving:
Calories: 301| Fat: 11.6g| Carbs: 31g| Fiber: 7.3g| Protein: 20.9g

2 tbsp. olive oil
1 bell pepper, seeded and chopped
1 small onion, chopped
2 garlic cloves, finely chopped
1 lb. lean ground turkey
1 (15-oz.) can sugar-free pumpkin puree
1 (14-oz.) can diced tomatoes with liquid
1 tsp. ground cumin
½ tsp. ground turmeric
½ tsp. ground cinnamon
1¼ C. water
1 (18-oz.) can chickpeas, drained

In a large-sized pan, heat oil over medium-low heat and sauté bell pepper, onion and garlic for about 5 minutes.
Add turkey and cook for about 5-6 minutes.
Add tomatoes, pumpkin, spices and water and cook until boiling over high heat.
Now adjust the heat to medium-low heat and stir in chickpeas.
Simmer, covered for about 30 minutes, stirring occasionally.
Serve hot.

ANTI-INFLAMMATORY DIET cookbook FOR BEGINNERS

Mixed Grains Chili

Prep Time: 15 mins.| Cook Time: 55 mins.| Serves: 12

2 tbsp. olive oil
2 shallots, chopped
1 large yellow onion, chopped
1 tbsp. fresh ginger root, finely grated
8 garlic cloves, minced
1 tsp. ground cumin
3 tbsp. red chili powder
Salt and ground black pepper, as required
1 (28-oz.) can crushed tomatoes
1 canned chipotle pepper, mince
1 Serrano pepper, seeded and finely chopped
2/3 C. bulgur wheat
2/3 C. pearl barley
2¼ C. mixed lentils (green, black, brown), rinsed
1½ C. canned chickpeas
3 scallions, chopped

In a large-sized Dutch oven, heat oil over medium heat and sauté shallot and onion for about 4-5 minutes.
Add ginger, garlic, cumin and chili powder and sauté for about 1 minute.
Stir in tomatoes, both peppers and broth.
Stir in the remaining ingredients except the scallion and bring to a rolling boil.
Immediately adjust the heat to low and simmer for about 35-45 minutes or until desired thickness of the chili.
Serve hot with the topping of scallion.

Per Serving:
Calories: 351|
Fat: 4.9g|
Carbs: 61g|
Fiber: 21.8g|
Protein: 18.6g

Meatballs Curry

Prep Time: 20 mins.| Cook Time: 22 mins.| Serves: 6

For Meatballs
1 lb. grass-fed lean ground beef
2 organic eggs, beaten
3 tbsp. red onion, minced
¼ C. fresh basil leaves, chopped
1 (1-inch) fresh ginger piece, finely chopped
4 garlic cloves, finely chopped
3 Serrano peppers, minced
1 tsp. coconut sugar
1 tbsp. red curry paste
Salt, as required
1 tbsp. red boat fish sauce
2 tbsp. coconut oil
For Curry
1 red onion, chopped
Salt, as required
4 garlic cloves, minced
1 (1-inch) fresh ginger piece, minced
2 Serrano peppers, minced
2 tbsp. red curry paste
1 (14-oz.) unsweetened coconut milk
Salt and ground black pepper, as required

For meatballs: in a large-sized bowl, add all ingredients except for oil and mix until well combined.
Make small-sized balls from mixture.
In a large-sized wok, melt coconut oil over medium heat and cook meatballs for about 3-5 minutes or until golden brown from all sides.
Transfer the meatballs into a bowl.
In the same wok, add onion and a pinch of salt and sauté for about 5 minutes.
Add garlic, ginger and chilies and sauté for about 1 minute.
Add curry paste and sauté for about 1 minute.
Add coconut milk and meatballs and bring to a gentle simmer.
Reduce the heat to low and simmer, covered for about 10 minutes.
Serve hot.

Per Serving:
Calories: 234| Fat: 14.9g|
Carbs: 6.8g| Fiber: 1.1g|
Protein: 18g

Spicy Lamb Curry

Prep Time: 15 mins.| Cook Time: 2 hrs. 20 mins.| Serves: 8

For Spice Mixture
2 tsp. ground coriander
2 tsp. ground cumin
2 tsp. ground cinnamon
¾ tsp. ground ginger
½ tsp. ground cloves
½ tsp. ground cardamom
2 tbsp. sweet paprika
½ tbsp. cayenne pepper
2 tsp. chili powder
2 tsp. salt
For Curry
1 tbsp. coconut oil
2 lb. boneless lamb, trimmed and cubed into 1-inch size
Salt and ground black pepper, as required
2 C. onions, chopped
1¼ C. water
1 C. coconut milk

For spice mixture: in a bowl, blend together all spices. Set aside.
Season the lamb with salt and black pepper.
In a large-sized Dutch oven, heat oil over medium-high heat and sear the lamb cubes for about 5 minutes.
Add onion and cook for about 4-5 minutes.
Stir in spice mixture and cook for about 1 minute.
Add in water and coconut milk and cook until boiling over high heat.
Now adjust the heat to low and simmer, covered for about 1-2 hours or until desired doneness of lamb.
Uncover and simmer for about 3-4 minutes.
Serve hot.

Per Serving:
Calories: 319|
Fat: 17.8g| Carbs: 6.9g| Fiber: 2.7g|
Protein: 33.4g

Fruity Shrimp Curry

Prep Time: 15 mins.| Cook Time: 15 mins.| Serves: 6

2 tsp. coconut oil, divided
½ C. onion, thinly sliced
1½ lb. shrimp, peeled and deveined
½ of red bell pepper, seeded and thinly sliced
1 mango, peeled, pitted and sliced
8 oz. can pineapple tidbits with unsweetened juice
1 C. unsweetened coconut milk
1 tbsp. red curry paste
2 tbsp. red boat fish sauce
2 tbsp. fresh cilantro, chopped

In a non-stick pan, melt 1 tsp. of coconut oil over medium-high heat and sauté onion for about 3-4 minutes.
With a spoon, push the onion to side of the pan.
Add the remaining coconut oil and shrimp and cook for about 2 minutes per side.
Add bell pepper and cook for about 3-4 minutes.
Add remaining ingredients except for cilantro and simmer for about 5 minutes.
Serve hot with the sprinkling of cilantro.

Per Serving:
Calories: 311| Fat: 14g|
Carbs: 19.7g| Fiber: 2.7g| Protein: 27.9g

ANTI-INFLAMMATORY DIET cookbook FOR BEGINNERS

Spicy Kidney Beans Curry

Prep Time: 10 mins.| Cook Time: 20 mins.| Serves: 6

¼ C. extra-virgin olive oil
1 medium onion, finely chopped
3 garlic cloves, mince
2 tbsp. fresh ginger, minced
1 (8-oz.) can sugar-free tomato sauce
1 tsp. ground coriander
1 tsp. ground cumin
½ tsp. ground turmeric
¼ tsp. cayenne pepper
Salt and ground black pepper, as required
1 (30-oz.) can red kidney beans with liquid
1 tomato, finely chopped
1 C. filtered water
½ C. fresh parsley, chopped

In a large-sized pan, heat the oil over medium heat.
Sauté the onion, garlic and ginger for about 2 minutes.
Stir in the tomato sauce and spices cook for about 2-3 minutes.
Stir in kidney beans with liquid, tomato and water and bring to a boil on high heat.
Reduce the heat to medium and simmer for about 10 minutes.
Serve hot with the garnishing of parsley.

Per Serving:
Calories: 221| Fat: 9.3g| Carbs: 28.4g| Fiber: 9.2g| Protein: 8.7g

Sea Bass With Veggies

Prep Time: 15 mins.| Cook Time: 15 mins.| Serves: 2

1 (8-oz.) sea bass fish fillet, cubed
¼ tsp. ginger paste
¼ tsp. garlic paste
1 tsp. red chili powder
Salt, as required
1 tbsp. coconut vinegar
1 tbsp. extra-virgin olive oil, divided
½ C. fresh mushrooms, sliced
1 small onion, quartered
¼ C. red bell pepper, seeded and cubed
¼ C. yellow bell pepper, seeded and cubed
2-3 scallions, chopped
1 tsp. red boat fish sauce

Per Serving:
Calories: 280| Fat: 17.6g| Carbs: 8.8g| Fiber: 2.2g| Protein: 23.9g

In a bowl, blend together fish, ginger, garlic, chili powder and salt and set aside for about 20 minutes.
In a non-stick wok, heat 1 tsp. of oil over medium-high heat and sear the fish for about 3-4 minutes or until golden from all sides.
In another wok, heat remaining oil over medium heat and stir fry the mushrooms and onion for about 5-7 minutes.
Add bell pepper and fish and stir fry for about 2 minutes.
Add scallion and fish sauce and stir fry for bout 1-2 minutes.
Serve hot.

SIDES & SALADS

RECIPES

Spicy Brussels Sprout

Prep Time: 10 mins.| Cook Time: 10 mins.| Serves: 4

2 tbsp. olive oil
1 tbsp. fresh ginger, minced
1 tbsp. garlic, minced
1 tbsp. dried fenugreek leaves
1 tbsp. cumin seeds
1 tsp. smoked paprika
Salt and ground black pepper, as required
1 lb. Brussels sprouts, trimmed and halved
½ C. filtered water

In a wok, heat the oil over medium heat and sauté the ginger and garlic for 1 minute.
Add the fenugreek leaves, cumin seeds, paprika, salt and black pepper and sauté for about 1 minute.
Stir in the Brussels sprouts and water and cook, covered for about 6-8 minutes.
Serve hot.

Per Serving:
Calories: 133| Fat: 8.1g| Carbs: 14.5g| Fiber: 5.5g| Protein: 5.1g

---

Turmeric Potatoes

Prep Time: 10 mins.| Cook Time: 14 mins.| Serves: 2

2 tbsp. olive oil
1 large potato, scrubbed and thinly sliced
1 garlic clove, minced
½ tsp. ground turmeric
Salt, as required
1 small onion, thinly sliced
1 tsp. fresh parsley, chopped

In a non-stick frying pan, heat the oil over medium heat and cook the potato slices, garlic, turmeric and salt for about 8-10 minutes, stirring frequently.
Add the onion and cook for about 4 minutes, stirring occasionally.
Serve hot with the garnishing f parsley.

Per Serving:
Calories: 380| Fat: 14.3g| Carbs: 36.4g| Fiber: 5g| Protein: 4.3g

Gingered Asparagus

Prep Time: 10 mins.| Cook Time: 6 mins.| Serves: 4

2 tbsp. olive oil
1 tsp. cumin seeds
1¼ lb. asparagus, trimmed and cut into 2-inch pieces diagonally
1 tbsp. fresh ginger, minced
2 tsp. fresh lemon juice
Salt and ground black pepper, as required

In a wok, heat oil over medium heat and sauté cumin seeds for about 1 minute.
Add remaining ingredients and stir fry for about 4-5 minutes.
Serve hot.

Per Serving:
Calories: 96| Fat: 7.4g| Carbs: 6.7g| Fiber: 3.2g| Protein: 3.4g

Sweet & Spicy Carrots

Prep Time: 10 mins.| Cook Time: 20 mins.| Serves: 3

1 lb. baby carrots, trimmed
1 tsp. fresh lime zest, finely grated
tsp. ground cumin
¼ tsp. smoked paprika
¼ tsp. ground coriander
Salt, as required
1 tsp. organic honey
2 tbsp. fresh lime juice
1 tbsp. olive oil
2 scallions, thinly sliced
2 tbsp. fresh mint leaves, chopped

Preheat your oven to 400 ºF.
In a baking dish, arrange the carrots.
In a large-sized bowl, mix together remaining ingredients except for scallion and mint.
Place the honey mixture over carrots evenly.
Roast for about 20 minutes.
Serve with the garnishing of scallion and mint.

Per Serving:
Calories: 109| Fat: 5.1g| Carbs: 16.1g| Fiber: 5.1g| Protein: 1.5g

Cabbage With Apple

Prep Time: 15 mins.| Cook Time: 10 mins.| Serves: 4

2 tsp. coconut oil
1 large apple, cored and thinly sliced
1 onion, thinly sliced
1½ lb. cabbage, finely chopped
1 tbsp. fresh thyme, chopped
1 red chili pepper, chopped
1 tbsp. apple cider vinegar
¼ C. almonds, chopped

In a non-stick wok, melt 1 tsp. of coconut oil over medium heat and stir fry the apple slices for about 2-3 minutes
Transfer the apple slices into a bowl
In the same wok, melt 1 tsp. of coconut oil over medium heat and sauté the onion for about 1-2 minutes.
Add the cabbage and stir fry for about 3-4 minutes.
Add the apple, thyme and vinegar and cook, covered for about 1 minute.
Serve warm with the garnishing of almonds.

Per Serving:
Calories: 139|
Fat: 5.6g| Carbs:
21.9g| Fiber:
7.2g| Protein: 4g

Citrus Greens Salad

Prep Time: 15 mins.| Serves: 2

For Salad
3 C. mix salad greens
1 orange, peeled and segmented
1 grapefruit, peeled and segmented
2 tbsp. unsweetened dried cranberries

For Dressing
2 tbsp. extra-virgin olive oil
2 tbsp. fresh orange juice
1 tsp. Dijon mustard
½ tsp. organic honey
Salt and ground black pepper, as required

For salad: in a salad bowl, place all ingredients and mix. For dressing: place all ingredients in another bowl and beat until well blended. Place dressing on top of salad and toss to coat well. Serve immediately.

Per Serving:
Calories: 256| Fat: 14.5g| Carbs: 31.3g|
Fiber: 4.8g| Protein: 4.8g

Mixed Fruit Salad

Prep Time: 15 mins.| Serves: 10

5 C. pineapple, peeled, cored and chopped
2 large mangoes, peeled, pitted and chopped
2 large Fuji apples, cored and chopped
2 large red Bartlett pears, cored and chopped
2 large navel oranges, peeled, seeded and sectioned
2 tsp. fresh ginger root, finely grated
2 tbsp. organic honey
¼ C. fresh lemon juice

In a bowl, blend together all fruits.
In a small-sized bowl, add remaining ingredients and beat well.
Place honey mixture over fruit mixture and toss to coat well.
Cover the bowl and refrigerate to chill completely before serving.

Per Serving:
Calories: 161| Fat: 0.6g|
Carbs: 41.6g| Fiber: 5.6g|
Protein: 1.7g

Greens & Seeds Salad

Prep Time: 15 mins.| Cook Time: 6 mins.| Serves: 4

1½ tsp. fresh ginger, finely grated
2 tbsp. apple cider vinegar
3 tbsp. olive oil
1 tsp. sesame oil, toasted
3 tsp. organic honey, divided
½ tsp. red pepper flakes, crushed and divided
Salt, as required
1 tbsp. water
2 tbsp. raw sunflower seeds
1 tbsp. raw sesame seeds
1 tbsp. raw pumpkin seeds
10 oz. collard greens, stems and ribs removed and thinly sliced

For dressing: in a bowl, add ginger, vinegar, both oils, 1 tsp. of honey, ¼ tsp. red pepper flakes and salt and beat until well combined. Set aside.
In another bowl, add the remaining honey, red pepper flakes and water and mix until well combined.
Heat a medium-sized non-stick wok over medium heat and cook all seeds for about 3 minutes, stirring continuously.
Stir in the honey mixture and cook, stirring continuously for about 3 minutes.
Transfer the seeds mixture onto parchment paper and set aside to cool completely.
Break the seeds mixture into small pieces.
In a large-sized bowl, add the greens, 2 tsp. of the dressing and a little salt and toss to coat well.
With your hands, rub the greens for about 30 seconds.
Add the remaining dressing and toss to coat well.
Serve with a garnishing of seeds pieces.

Per Serving:
Calories: 184|
Fat: 15.6g| Carbs:
10.5g| Fiber:
2.1g| Protein:
3.6g

Beans & Mango Salad

Prep Time: 15 mins.| Serves: 6

For Salad
2 (15½-oz.) cans black beans, drained
2 mangoes, peeled, pitted and chopped
½ C. red onion, chopped
2 tbsp. fresh cilantro, chopped

For Dressing
1 (½-inch) piece fresh ginger, grated
2 tsp. fresh orange zest, finely grated
3-4 tbsp. fresh orange juice
1 tbsp. apple cider vinegar
2 tsp. extra-virgin olive oil
¼ tsp. red pepper flakes, crushed

For salad: in a large-sized bowl, add all the ingredients and mix.
For dressing: in another bowl, add all the ingredients and beat until well combined.
Place the dressing over beans mixture and mix until well combined.
Serve immediately.

Per Serving:
Calories: 291| Fat: 2.9g| Carbs: 55.3g| Fiber: 15.3g| Protein: 14.4g

---

Chicken Salad

Prep Time: 15 mins.| Cook Time: 15 mins.| Serves: 4

For Chicken
4 (4-oz.) skinless, boneless chicken breast halves, trimmed
2 tsp. orange zest, finely grated
1/3 C. fresh orange juice
4 garlic cloves, minced
1 tbsp. fresh ginger root, minced
2 tbsp. maple syrup
1½ tsp. dried thyme, crushed

For Salad
6 C. fresh arugula
2 C. cherry tomatoes, quartered
3 tbsp. extra-virgin olive oil
2 tbsp. fresh lemon juice
Salt and ground black pepper, as required

Per Serving: Calories: 300| Fat: 15.1g| Carbs: 15.3g| Fiber: 2g| Protein: 27.3g

For chicken: in a Zip lock bag, all the ingredients.
Seal the Zip lock bag tightly and shake to coat well.
Refrigerate to marinate for about 6-8 hours, flipping occasionally.
Preheat your oven to broiler.
Line a broiler pan with a piece of foil.
Arrange the oven rack about 6-inch away from heating element.
Remove the chicken breasts from bag and discard the marinade.
Arrange the chicken breasts onto the prepared pan in a single layer.
Broil for about for 15 minutes, flipping once halfway through.
. Remove the chicken breasts from oven and place onto a cutting board for about 10 minutes.
. Cut the chicken breasts into desired-sized slices.
. For salad: in a bowl, add all ingredients and toss to coat well.
. Add chicken slices and stir to combine.
. Serve immediately.

VEGETABLES &

VEGAN RECIPES

Pumpkin Curry

Prep Time: 15 mins.| Cook Time: 35 mins.| Serves: 4

For Roasted Pumpkin
1 medium sugar pumpkin, peeled and cubed
Salt, as required
1 tsp. extra-virgin olive oil

For Curry
1 tsp. extra-virgin olive oil
1 onion, chopped
1 tbsp. fresh ginger root, minced
1 tbsp. garlic, minced
1 C. coconut milk
2 C. homemade vegetable broth
1 tbsp. curry powder
1 tsp. ground cumin
½ tsp. ground turmeric
Salt and ground black pepper, as required
1 tbsp. fresh lime juice
2 tbsp. fresh parsley, chopped

Preheat your oven to 400 ºF.
Line a large-sized baking sheet with baking paper.
For roasted pumpkin: in a bowl, add all ingredients and toss to coat well.
Place pumpkin onto prepared baking sheet in a single layer.
Roast for 20-25 minutes, flipping once halfway through.
Meanwhile, in a large-sized pan, heat oil over medium-high heat and sauté onion for 4-5 minutes.
Stir in the ginger and garlic and sauté for about 1 minute.
Add coconut milk, broth, spices, salt, and black pepper and bring to a rolling boil.
Now adjust the heat to low and simmer for 10 minutes.
. Stir in the roasted pumpkin and simmer for 10 more minutes.
. Serve hot with a garnish of parsley.

Per Serving:
Calories: 263| Fat: 18.3g|
Carbs: 23.4g| Fiber: 7.8g|
Protein: 6.6g

Mixed Veggie Curry

Prep Time: 15 mins.| Cook Time: 30 mins.| Serves: 4

Per Serving:
Calories: 359| Fat: 27.8g|
Carbs: 28.2g|
Fiber: 8.6g|
Protein: 6.3g

1 tbsp. coconut oil
1 green bell pepper, seeded and chopped
1 onion, chopped
1 C. homemade pumpkin puree
1 tbsp. curry powder
1 tsp. ground cinnamon
¼ tsp. ground ginger
Salt, as required
1 (14-oz.) can unsweetened coconut milk
1 C. water
1 sweet potato, peeled and cubed into 1-inch size
1 head broccoli, cut into florets

In a large-sized pan, melt coconut oil over medium heat and cook onion for about 8 minutes, stirring frequently.
Add the pumpkin puree, curry powder, cinnamon, ginger, salt, coconut milk and water and stir to combine well.
Stir in the sweet potato and broccoli and bring to a gentle simmer.
Simmer, covered for about 15-20 minutes.
Serve hot.

Cashew Veggie Stew

Prep Time: 15 mins.| Cook Time: 30 mins.| Serves: 4

2 tbsp. olive oil
1 large onion, chopped
2 garlic cloves, minced
¼ tsp. fresh ginger, finely grated
1 tsp. ground cumin
1 tsp. cayenne pepper
Salt and ground black pepper, as required
2 C. homemade vegetable broth
1½ C. small broccoli florets
1½ C. small cauliflower florets
1 tbsp. fresh lemon juice
½ C. cashews
1 tsp. fresh lemon zest, finely grated

Per Serving:
Calories: 221|
Fat: 16.1g|
Carbs: 15.1g|
Fiber: 3.4g|
Protein: 7.4g

Add 1 C. of the broth and bring to a boil. Add the vegetables and again bring to a boil. Cover the soup pan and cook for about 15-20 minutes, stirring occasionally.
Stir in the lemon juice and serve hot with the topping of cashews and lemon zest.
In a large-sized soup pan, heat oil over medium heat and sauté the onion for about 3-4 minutes.
Add the garlic, ginger and spices and sauté for about 1 minute.

Spinach, Mushrooms & Tomato Combo

Prep Time: 15 mins.| Cook Time: 15 mins.| Serves: 2

1 tsp. coconut oil
5-6 button mushrooms, sliced
2 tbsp. olive oil
½ of red onion, sliced
1 garlic clove, minced
½ tsp. fresh lemon rind, finely grated
¼ C. cherry tomatoes, halved
Salt and ground black pepper, as required
Pinch of ground nutmeg
3 C. fresh spinach, torn
½ tbsp. fresh lemon juice

In a medium-sized wok, melt coconut oil over medium heat and sauté mushrooms for about 3-4 minutes.
With a slotted spoon, transfer the mushrooms into a bowl and set aside.
In the same wok, heat olive oil over medium heat and sauté onion for about 2-3 minutes.
Add garlic, lemon rind and tomatoes, salt and black pepper and cook for about 2-3 minutes, smashing the tomatoes slightly with a spatula.
Stir in spinach and cook for about 2-3 minutes.
Stir in mushrooms and lemon juice and remove from heat.
Serve hot.

Per Serving:
Calories: 179|
Fat: 16.8g| Carbs: 7.3g| Fiber: 2.4g|
Protein: 3.4g

ANTI-INFLAMMATORY DIET cookbook FOR BEGINNERS

Veggie Kabobs

Prep Time: 15 mins.| Cook Time: 15 mins.| Serves: 5

For Marinade
3 garlic cloves, chopped
1 (1-inch) piece fresh ginger, chopped
1 tsp. ground cumin
1 tsp. ground coriander
1 tsp. sweet paprika
1/8 tsp. red chili powder
Salt and ground black pepper, as required
¼ C. fresh lemon juice
¼ C. olive oil
½ bunch of fresh cilantro
½ bunch of fresh parsley

For Vegetables
Olive oil cooking spray
2 medium red bell pepper, seeded and cut into 1-inch pieces
2 medium zucchinis, cut into 1/3-inch thick round slices
1 lb. fresh button mushrooms
1 large onion, sliced into 1-inch pieces
1 large eggplant, quartered lengthwise and cut into ½-inch thick slices diagonally

For marinade: in a food processor, add all ingredients except for herbs and pulse until well combined
Add fresh herbs and pulse until smooth.
In a large-sized bowl, add vegetables and marinade and toss to coat well.
Refrigerate, covered for about 4 hours.
Preheat the grill to medium-low heat.
Grease the grill grate with cooking spray.
Thread the vegetables onto pre-soaked wooden skewers.
Place the skewers onto the grill and cook for about 15 minutes, flipping occasionally.
Serve hot.

Per Serving:
Calories: 181| Fat: 11.1g| Carbs: 19.5g| Fiber: 6.7g| Protein: 6g

Quinoa With Asparagus

Prep Time: 10 mins.| Cook Time: 18 mins.| Serves: 4

Per Serving: Calories: 258| Fat: 5.8g| Carbs: 38.8g| Fiber: 10.9g| Protein: 17.3g

1 lb. fresh asparagus, trimmed
2 tsp. coconut oil
½ of onion, chopped
2 garlic cloves, minced
1 C. cooked red quinoa
1 tbsp. ground turmeric
½ C. homemade vegetable broth
½ C. nutritional yeast
1 tbsp. fresh lemon juice

In a large-sized pan of boiling water, cook the asparagus for about 2-3 minutes.
Drain the asparagus well and rinse under cold water.
In a large-sized wok, melt the coconut oil over medium heat and sauté the onion and garlic for about 5 minutes.
Stir in the quinoa, turmeric and broth and cook for about 5-6 minutes.
Stir in the nutritional yeast, lemon juice and asparagus and cook for about 3-4 minutes.
Serve hot.

Three Beans Chili

Prep Time: 15 mins.| Cook Time: 1 hr.| Serves: 6

2 tbsp. olive oil
1 green bell pepper, seeded and chopped
2 celery stalks, chopped
1 scallion, chopped
3 garlic cloves, minced
1 tsp. dried oregano, crushed
1 tbsp. red chili powder
2 tsp. ground cumin
1 tsp. red pepper flakes, crushed
1 tsp. paprika
1 tsp. ground turmeric
1 tsp. onion powder
1 tsp. garlic powder
Salt and ground black pepper, as required
4½ C. plum tomatoes, finely chopped
4 C. water
16 oz. canned cannellini beans, drained and rinsed
16 oz. canned kidney beans, drained and rinsed
½ of (16-oz.) can black beans, drained and rinsed
1 jalapeño pepper, seeded and chopped

In a large-sized pan, heat oil over medium heat and cook the bell peppers, celery, scallion and garlic for about 8-10 minutes, stirring frequently.
Add the oregano, spices, salt, black pepper, tomatoes and water and bring to a rolling boil.
Simmer for about 20 minutes.
Stir in the beans and jalapeño pepper and simmer for about 30 minutes.
Serve hot.

Per Serving:
Calories: 342|
Fat: 6.1g|
Carbs: 56g|
Fiber: 21.3g|
Protein: 20.3g

Beans & Veggie Soup

Prep Time: 15 mins.| Cook Time: 55 mins.| Serves: 4

2 tsp. extra-virgin olive oil
1 medium onion, chopped
4 garlic cloves, minced
1 tbsp. fresh ginger root, minced
2 tsp. fresh rosemary, minced
1 lb. sweet potatoes, peeled and cut into small cubes
4 C. water
1 tsp. ground turmeric
1 tsp. ground cumin
Salt and ground black pepper, as required
15 oz. canned white beans, rinsed and drained
3 C. fresh kale, tough ribs removed and chopped roughly

In a large-sized pan, heat the oil over medium heat and cook the onions for about 7-9 minutes, stirring frequently.
Add the garlic, ginger and rosemary and sauté for about 1 minute.
Add the potatoes, water, spices, salt and black pepper and bring to a rolling boil.
Adjust the heat to low and simmer, uncovered for about 30-35 minutes.
With the back of a spoon, mash some of the potatoes roughly.
Stir in the beans and kale and simmer for about 4-7 minutes.
Serve hot.

Per Serving:
Calories: 289|
Fat: 3.2g|
Carbs: 54.7g|
Fiber: 15.6g|
Protein: 12.7g

Lentil & Quinoa Stew

Prep Time: 15 mins.| Cook Time: 30 mins.| Serves: 6

1 tbsp. coconut oil
3 carrots, peeled and chopped
3 celery stalks, chopped
1 yellow onion, chopped
4 garlic cloves, minced
4 C. tomatoes, chopped
1 C. red lentils, rinsed and drained
½ C. dried quinoa, rinsed and drained
1½ tsp. ground cumin
1 tsp. red chili powder
5 C. homemade vegetable broth
2 C. fresh spinach, chopped
Salt and ground black pepper, as required

In a large-sized pan, heat the oil over medium heat and sauté the celery, onion, and carrot for about 4-5 minutes.
Add the garlic and sauté for about 1 minute.
Add the remaining ingredients except for the spinach and bring to a rolling boil.
Now adjust the heat to low and simmer, covered for about 20 minutes
.Stir in spinach and simmer for about 3-4 minutes.
Stir in the salt and black pepper and remove from heat.
Serve hot.

Per Serving:
Calories: 292| Fat: 6.9g| Carbs: 39.1g| Fiber: 17.1g| Protein: 19g

Chickpeas & Veggie Curry

Prep Time: 15 mins.| Cook Time: 25 mins.| Serves: 3

¼ C. onion, chopped
1 (1-inch) piece fresh ginger, chopped
4 garlic cloves, chopped
2-3 tbsp. water
1 tsp. olive oil
½ tsp. ground coriander
½ tsp. ground cumin
½ tsp. ground turmeric
¼ tsp. ground cardamom
¼ tsp. ground cinnamon
1/3 tsp. cayenne pepper
½ C. unsweetened coconut milk
3 tbsp. almond butter
¾ C. homemade vegetable broth
1 (15-oz.) can chickpeas, rinsed and drained
½ C. zucchini, sliced
½ C. carrot, peeled and sliced
½ of red bell pepper, seeded and sliced
¼ tsp. red pepper flakes, crushed
Salt and ground black pepper, as required
1 tsp. fresh lime juice
2 tbsp. fresh cilantro, chopped

In a clean blender, add onion, ginger, garlic and water and pulse until smooth.
In a medium-sized pan, heat oil over medium heat and sauté spices for about 30 seconds.
Add onion mixture and sauté for about 7-9 minutes.
Add coconut milk and almond butter and stir to combine well.
Increase the heat to medium-high.
Stir in broth, chickpeas, vegetables, red pepper flakes, salt and black pepper and bring to a rolling boil.
Now adjust the heat to medium-low and simmer for about 5 minutes.
Stir in lime juice and cilantro and simmer for about 3-4 minutes.
Serve hot.

Per Serving:
Calories: 335| Fat: 14g| Carbs: 43.6g| Fiber: 8.8g| Protein: 11.9g

FISH & SEAFOOD

RECIPES

Poached Salmon

Prep Time: 10 mins.| Cook Time: 15 mins.| Serves: 3

3 garlic cloves, crushed
1 tsp. fresh ginger root, finely grated
1/3 C. fresh orange juice
3 tbsp. coconut aminos
3 (6-oz.) salmon fillets

In a large-sized bowl, add all ingredients except for salmon fillets and mix until well blended.
In the bottom of a large-sized pan, place the salmon fillets
Place the ginger mixture over the salmon evenly and set aside in room temperature for about 15 minutes.
Place the pan over high heat and bring to a rolling boil.
Now adjust the heat to low and simmer, covered for about 10-12 minutes or until desired doneness.
Serve hot.

Per Serving:
Calories: 259| Fat: 10.6g| Carbs: 7.3g| Fiber: 0.2g| Protein: 33.4g

Walnut Crusted Salmon

Prep Time: 15 mins.| Cook Time: 20 mins.| Serves: 4

1 C. walnuts
1 tbsp. fresh dill, chopped
2 tbsp. fresh lemon zest, grated
½ tsp. garlic salt
Freshly ground black pepper, as required
1 tbsp. olive oil
3-4 tbsp. Dijon mustard
4 (3-oz.) salmon fillets
4 tsp. fresh lemon juice

Preheat your oven to 350 °F.
Line a large-sized baking sheet with parchment paper.
In a food processor, place the walnuts and pulse until chopped roughly.
Add the dill, lemon rind, garlic salt, black pepper, and butter and pulse until a crumbly mixture forms.
Place the salmon fillets onto the prepared baking sheet in a single layer, skin-side down.
Coat the top of each salmon fillet with Dijon mustard.
Place the walnut mixture over each fillet and gently press into the surface of salmon.
Bake for approximately 15-20 minutes.
Remove the salmon fillets from oven and transfer onto the serving plates.
. Drizzle with lemon juice and serve.

Per Serving:
Calories: 350|
Fat: 27.8g|
Carbs: 5.2g|
Fiber: 2.9g|
Protein: 24.9g

Honey Salmon

Prep Time: 10 mins.| Cook Time: 12 mins.| Serves: 2

2 (6-oz.) salmon fillets
2 tbsp. plus ½ tsp. organic honey, divided
1/3 tsp. ground turmeric, divided
Freshly ground black pepper, as required
2 large lemon slices

In a Zip lock bag, add salmon, ½ tsp. of honey, ¼ tsp. of turmeric and black pepper.
Seal the Zip lock bag tightly and shake to coat well.
Refrigerate to marinate for about 1 hour.
Preheat your oven to 400 ºF.
Transfer the salmon fillets onto a baking sheet in a single layer.
Cover the fillets with marinade.
Place the salmon fillets, skin-side up and bake for approximately 6 minutes.
Carefully change the side of fillets.
Sprinkle with remaining turmeric and black pepper evenly.
. Place 1 lemon slice over each fillet and drizzle with remaining honey.
. Bake for approximately 6 minutes.
. Serve hot.

Per Serving:
Calories: 290| Fat: 10.5g| Carbs: 17.6g| Fiber: 0.1g| Protein: 33.1g

Salmon In Yogurt Sauce

Prep Time: 15 mins.| Cook Time: 35 mins.| Serves: 5

5 (4-oz.) salmon steaks
1½ tsp. ground turmeric, divided
Salt, as required
3 tbsp. coconut oil, divided
1 (1-inch) stick cinnamon, pounded roughly
3-4 green cardamom, pounded roughly
4-5 whole cloves, pounded roughly
2 bay leaves
1 onion, finely chopped
1 tsp. garlic paste
1½ tsp. ginger paste
3-4 green chili peppers, halved
1 tsp. red chili powder
¾ C. plain Greek yogurt
¾ C. water
¼ C. fresh cilantro, chopped

In a bowl, season the salmon with ½ tsp. of the turmeric and salt and set aside.
In a large-sized wok, melt 1 tbsp. of coconut oil over medium heat and cook the salmon for about 2 minutes per side.
Transfer the salmon into a bowl.
In the same wok, melt remaining oil over medium heat and sauté cinnamon, green cardamom, whole cloves and bay leaves for about 1 minute.
Add onion and sauté for about 4-5 minutes.
Add garlic paste, ginger paste, green chilies and sauté for about 2 minutes.
Now adjust the heat to medium-low.
Add remaining turmeric, red chili powder and salt and sauté for about 1 minute.
Meanwhile, in a bowl, add yogurt and water and beat until smooth.
Now, adjust the heat to low and Slowly add the yogurt mixture, stirring continuously.
Simmer, covered for about 15 minutes.
Carefully add the salmon fillets and simmer for about 5 minutes.
Serve hot with the topping of cilantro.

Per Serving:
Calories: 270| Fat: 16g| Carbs: 7.3g| Fiber: 1.4g| Protein: 24.8g

ANTI-INFLAMMATORY DIET cookbook FOR BEGINNERS

Cod In Tomato Sauce

Prep Time: 15 mins.| Cook Time: 35 mins.| Serves: 5

1 tsp. dried dill weed
2 tsp. sumac
2 tsp. ground coriander
1½ tsp. ground cumin
1 tsp. ground turmeric
2 tbsp. olive oil
1 large sweet onion, chopped
8 garlic cloves, chopped
2 jalapeño peppers, chopped
5 medium tomatoes, chopped
3 tbsp. tomato paste
2 tbsp. fresh lime juice
½ C. water
Salt and ground black pepper, as required
5 (6-oz.) cod fillets

For spice mixture: in a small-sized bowl, add the dill weed and spices and mix well.
In a large-sized, deep wok, heat the oil over medium-high heat and sauté the onion for about 2 minutes.
Add the garlic and jalapeno and sauté for about 2 minutes.
Stir in the tomatoes, tomato paste, lime juice, water, half of the spice mixture, salt and pepper and bring to a rolling boil.
Adjust the heat to medium-low and cook, covered for about 10 minutes, stirring occasionally.
Meanwhile, season the cod fillets with the remaining spice mixture, salt and pepper evenly.
Place the fish fillets into the wok and gently press into the tomato mixture.
Adjust the heat to medium-high and cook for about 2 minutes.
Adjust the heat to medium and cook, covered for about 10-15 minutes or until desired doneness of the fish.
Serve hot.

Per Serving:
Calories: 301| Fat: 7.9g| Carbs: 12.2g| Fiber: 3g| Protein: 45.2g

Gingered Tilapia

Prep Time: 10 mins.| Cook Time: 6 mins.| Serves: 5

Per Serving:
Calories: 266| Fat: 8.8g| Carbs: 19.9g| Fiber: 3.7g| Protein: 29.1g

2 tbsp. coconut oil
5 (5-oz.) tilapia fillets
3 garlic cloves, minced
2 tbsp. fresh ginger root, minced
2 tbsp. unsweetened coconut, shredded
2 tbsp. coconut aminos
8 scallions, chopped

In a large-sized wok, melt coconut oil over medium heat and cook tilapia fillets for about 2 minutes.
Flip the side and add garlic, coconut and ginger and cook for about 1 minute.
Add coconut aminos and cook for about 1 minute.
Add scallion and cook for about 1-2 minute more.
Serve immediately.

Halibut Kabobs

Prep Time: 15 mins.| Cook Time: 8 mins.| Serves: 6

1 tbsp. arrowroot starch
2 C. fresh pineapple juice
2 tbsp. coconut aminos
1½ tbsp. balsamic vinegar
3 tbsp. fresh ginger, minced
2 garlic cloves, crushed
1¼ lb. halibut, cut into chunk
4 C. fresh pineapple, cut into large chunks
1 large onion, cut into wedges

In a small-sized pan, dissolve arrowroot starch in pineapple juice.
Add the coconut aminos, vinegar, ginger and garlic and simmer for about 7 minutes.
Remove from heat and set aside to cool.
Transfer the sauce mixture into a bowl.
Add the fish chunks and pineapple and mix well.
Refrigerate for about 30 minutes.
Preheat the broiler of oven. Arrange oven rack about 6-inch from the heating element. Arrange a rack onto a broiling pan
Thread fish, pineapple and onion onto metal skewers.
Arrange the skewers onto the prepared broiler pan and broil for about 2-4 minutes per side, coating with remaining marinade occasionally.
. Remove the skewers from the oven and serve immediately.

Per Serving: Calories: 235| Fat: 2.6g| Carbs: 31.9g| Fiber: 2.6g| Protein: 21.4g

---

Snapper Parcel

Prep Time: 10 mins.| Cook Time: 10 mins.| Serves: 2

Per Serving: Calories: 390| Fat: 17.5g| Carbs: 10.1g| Fiber: 1.2g| Protein: 45.1g

2 tbsp. garlic, minced
1 tbsp. fresh turmeric, finely grated
1 tbsp. fresh ginger root, finely grated
2 tbsp. fresh lime juice
2 tbsp. coconut aminos
2 tbsp. olive oil
1 bunch fresh cilantro, chopped
2 (6-oz.) snapper fillets

In a food processor, add garlic, turmeric, ginger, lime juice, coconut aminos and olive oil and pulse until smooth.
Transfer the mixture in a bowl with cilantro and mix well.
Add snapper fillets and coat with the mixture generously.
Place each fish fillet in the center of a piece of foil.
Wrap the foil around fish to form a parcel.
Arrange a steamer basket in a pan of boiling water.
Place the parcels in steamer basket.
Cover and steam for about 10 minutes.
Serve hot.

ANTI-INFLAMMATORY DIET cookbook FOR BEGINNERS

Prawns With Asparagus

Prep Time: 15 mins.| Cook Time: 11 mins.| Serves: 4

2 tbsp. olive oil
1 lb. fresh asparagus, peeled and chopped
1 lb. prawns, peeled and deveined
4 garlic cloves, minced
½ tsp. ground ginger
2 tbsp. fresh lemon juice
2/3 C. homemade chicken broth

In a large-sized wok, melt coconut oil over medium-high heat.
Add all ingredients except for broth and cook for about 2 minutes, without stirring.
Stir and cook for about 5 minutes.
Add broth and cook for about 2-4 minutes.
Serve hot.

Per Serving:
Calories: 231| Fat: 9.4g| Carbs: 7.6g|
Fiber: 2.5g| Protein: 29.4g

Shrimp & Veggie Curry

Prep Time: 15 mins.| Cook Time: 15 mins.| Serves: 6

2 tsp. coconut oil
1½ medium onions, sliced
1 tbsp. fresh ginger root, finely grated
2 medium bell peppers, sliced
3 medium carrots, peeled and sliced
1½ lb. medium shrimp, peeled and deveined
3 garlic cloves, minced
2½ tsp. curry powder
1½ tbsp. red boat fish sauce
1 C. unsweetened coconut milk
Water, as required
Salt, as required

In a non-stick pan, melt 1 tsp. of coconut oil over medium-high heat and sauté onion for about 3-4 minutes.
With a spoon, push the onion to side of the pan.
Add the remaining coconut oil and shrimp and cook for about 2 minutes per side.
Add bell peppers and cook for about 3-4 minutes.
Add remaining ingredients except for cilantro and simmer for about 5 minutes.
Serve hot with the sprinkling of cilantro.

Per Serving:
Calories: 311|
Fat: 14g| Carbs:
19.7g| Fiber:
2.7g| Protein:
27.9g

POULTRY & RED

MEAT RECIPES

Spiced Whole Chicken

Prep Time: 15 mins.| Cook Time: 1 hr.| Serves: 6

1 tsp. ground ginger
½ tsp. ground cumin
½ tsp. ground coriander
1 tsp. paprika
Salt and ground black pepper, as required
1 (3-lb.) whole chicken, neck and giblets removed
4 medium carrots, peeled and cut into 2-inch pieces
2 medium sweet potatoes, peeled and cut into ½-inch wedges
½ C. water

Preheat your oven to 450 ºF.
In a small-sized bowl, blend together the spices.
Rub the chicken with spice mixture evenly.
Arrange the chicken in a large-sized Dutch oven and place carrot and sweet potato pieces around it.
Add water and cover the pan tightly.
Roast for approximately 30 minutes.
Uncover and roast for approximately 30 minutes.
Remove the pan from oven and place the chicken onto a cutting board for about 10 minutes before carving.
Cut the chicken into desired-sized pieces and serve.

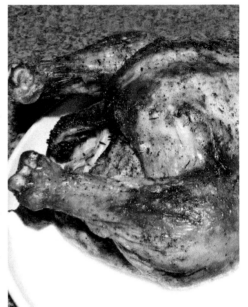

Per Serving:
Calories: 514| Fat: 32.6g| Carbs: 16.1g| Fiber: 2.9g| Protein: 39.6g

Chicken With Mango & Cashews

Prep Time: 15 mins.| Cook Time: 18 mins.| Serves: 4

2 tbsp. coconut oil
2 (8-oz.) skinless, boneless chicken breasts, sliced
1 red onion, thinly sliced
2 garlic cloves, minced
2 tbsp. fresh ginger root, minced
1 ripe mango, peeled, pitted and cubed
1 bunch broccoli, cut into small florets
1 zucchini, sliced
1 C. mushrooms, sliced
1 red bell pepper, seeded and cubed
3 tbsp. coconut aminos
¼ tsp. red pepper flakes, crushed
Salt and ground black pepper, as required
¼ C. cashews, toasted

Per Serving:
Calories: 374| Fat: 15.8g| Carbs: 30.8g| Fiber: 5.2g| Protein: 31g

In a large-sized wok, melt coconut oil over medium-high heat and stir fry chicken for about 4-5 minutes or until golden brown.
With a slotted spoon, transfer the chicken onto a plate.
In the same wok, add onion, garlic and ginger and sauté for about 1-2 minutes.
Add mango, broccoli, zucchini and bell pepper and cook for about 5-7 minutes.
Add chicken, beans sprouts, coconut aminos, red pepper flakes, salt and black pepper and cook for about 3-4 minutes or until desired doneness.
Serve with the topping of cashews.

Ground Turkey With Asparagus

Prep Time: 15 mins.| Cook Time: 20 mins.| Serves: 8

1¾ pounds lean ground turkey
2 tablespoons sesame oil
1 medium onion, chopped
1 cup celery, chopped
6 garlic cloves, minced
2 cups fresh asparagus, trimmed and cut into 1-inch pieces
1/3 cup coconut aminos
2 teaspoons ginger powder
2 tablespoons organic coconut crystals
1 tablespoon arrowroot starch
1 tablespoon cold water
¼ teaspoon red pepper flakes, crushed

I
Heat a large-sized non-stick wok over medium-high heat and cook turkey for about 6-8 minutes or until browned.
With a slotted spoon transfer the turkey into a bowl and discard the grease from wok.
In the same wok, heat oil over medium heat and sauté onion, celery and garlic for about 5 minutes.
Stir in the asparagus and cooked turkey and stir to combine.
Now adjust the heat to medium-low and cook or about 2-3 minutes.
Meanwhile, for sauce: in a small pan blend together coconut aminos, ginger powder and coconut crystals over medium heat and bring to a rolling boil.
In a small bowl, blend together arrowroot starch and water.
Slowly add the arrowroot mixture in sauce, stirring continuously.
Cook for about 2-3 minutes.
Add the sauce in wok with turkey mixture and stir to combine.
Stir in red pepper flakes and cook for about 3-4 minutes.
Serve hot

Per Serving:
Calories: 216| Fat: 10.6g| Carbs: 10g| Fiber: 1.4g| Protein: 20.7g

Duck With Bok Choy

Prep Time: 15 mins.| Cook Time: 13 mins.| Serves: 6

2 tbsp. coconut oil
1 yellow onion, thinly sliced
2 tsp. fresh ginger root, finely grated
2 garlic cloves, minced
1 tbsp. orange zest, finely grated
¼ C. homemade chicken broth
2/3 C. fresh orange juice
1½ lb. cooked duck meat, chopped
2 lb. baby bok choy
1 large orange, peeled, seeded and segmented

In a large-sized wok, melt coconut oil over medium heat and sauté onion, ginger and garlic for about 3 minutes
Add ginger and garlic and sauté for about 1-2 minutes.
Add the orange zest, broth and orange juice and bring to a rolling boil.
Add duck meat and cook for about 3 minutes.
Transfer the meat pieces onto a plate.
Add bok choy and cook for about 3-4 minutes.
Divide bok choy mixture in serving plates and top with duck meat.
Serve with the garnishing of orange segments.

Per Serving:
Calories: 317| Fat: 10.6g| Carbs: 12.2g| Fiber: 3.7g| Protein: 31g

Glazed Flank Steak

Prep Time: 15 mins.| Cook Time: 20 mins.| Serves: 6

2 tbsp. arrowroot flour
Salt and ground black pepper, as required
1½ lb. grass-fed flank steak, trimmed and cut into ¼-inch thick slices
5 tbsp. extra-virgin olive oil, divided
1 yellow onion, sliced
2 garlic cloves, minced
1 tsp. fresh ginger root, minced
¼ tsp. ground cumin
1/3 C. maple syrup
½ C. homemade beef broth
½ C. coconut aminos
2 tbsp. fresh lemon juice
¼ C. cashews
2 tbsp. fresh parsley, chopped

In a large-sized bowl, blend together arrowroot flour, salt and black pepper. Coat the beef slices in arrowroot flour mixture evenly and then shake off excess mixture.

Set aside for about 10-15 minutes.

For sauce: in a small-sized saucepan, heat 1 tablespoon of oil over medium heat and sauté the onion for about 3-4 minutes.

Add garlic, ginger and cumin and sauté for about 1 minute.

Add the maple syrup, broth and coconut aminos and stir to combine well.

Adjust the heat to high and cook for about 3 minutes, stirring continuously. Remove the pan of sauce from heat and set aside.

In a large-sized wok, heat remaining oil over medium-high heat and fry the beef slices for about 3-4 minutes.

. With a slotted spoon, transfer the beef slices onto a paper towel-lined plate to drain.

. Remove the oil from sauté pan, leaving about 1 tablespoon inside.

. Return the beef slices into sauté pan over medium heat and sear the beef slices for about 2-3 minutes.

. Stir in sauce and cook for about 3-5 minutes.

. Stir in the lemon juice and serve hot with the garnishing of cashews and parsley.

Per Serving:
Calories: 385| Fat: 21.6g| Carbs: 20.3g| Fiber: 0.7g| Protein: 26.8g

Beef With Broccoli

Prep Time: 10 mins.| Cook Time: 15 mins.| Serves: 6

Per Serving:
Calories: 205| Fat: 9.9g| Carbs: 3.9g| Fiber: 1.6g| Protein: 24.7g

2 tbsp. coconut oil, divided
2 garlic cloves, minced
1 lb. beef sirloin steak, trimmed and cut into thin strips
Salt, as required
¼ C. homemade chicken broth
2 tsp. fresh ginger root, grated
1 tbsp. ground flaxseeds
½ tsp. red pepper flakes, crushed
Salt and ground black pepper, as required
3 C. broccoli florets

In a large-sized wok, melt 1 tbsp. of coconut oil over medium-high heat and sauté garlic for about 1 minute.
Add beef and salt and cook for about 4-5 minutes or until browned.
With a slotted spoon, transfer the beef into a bowl.
Remove the excess liquid from wok.
In a bowl, blend together broth, ginger, flaxseed, red pepper flakes, salt and black pepper.
Melt remaining coconut oil in the same wok over medium heat and cook the broccoli and ginger mixture for about 3-4 minutes.
Stir in the cooked beef and cook for about 3-4 minutes.
Serve hot.

Pork With Pineapple

Prep Time: 15 mins.| Cook Time: 14 mins.| Serves: 6

2 tbsp. coconut oil
1½ lb. pork tenderloin, trimmed and cut into bite-sized pieces
1 onion, chopped
2 garlic cloves, minced
1 (1-inch) piece fresh ginger, minced
20 oz. pineapple, cut into chunks
1 large red bell pepper, seeded and chopped
¼ C. fresh pineapple juice
¼ C. coconut aminos
Ground black pepper, as required

In a large-sized wok, melt the coconut oil over high heat and stir fry the pork pieces for about 4-5 minutes
Transfer the pork pieces into a bowl
In the same wok, heat the remaining oil over medium heat and sauté the onion, garlic and ginger for about 2 minutes.
Stir in the pineapple and bell pepper and stir fry for about 3 minutes
Stir in the pork, pineapple juice, coconut aminos and black pepper and cook for about 3-4 minutes.
Serve hot.

Per Serving:
Calories: 282| Fat: 8.8g| Carbs: 19.8g| Fiber: 2.1g| Protein: 30.8g

ANTI-INFLAMMATORY DIET cookbook FOR BEGINNERS

Pork Chops With Peach

Prep Time: 15 mins.| Cook Time: 20 mins.| Serves: 2

2 boneless pork chops
Salt and ground black pepper, as required
1 ripe yellow peach, peeled, pitted, chopped and divided
1 tbsp. olive oil
2 tbsp. shallot, minced
2 tbsp. garlic, minced
2 tbsp. fresh ginger, minced
1 tbsp. organic honey
1 tbsp. balsamic vinegar
1 tbsp. coconut aminos
¼ tsp. red pepper flakes, crushed
¼ C. water

Per Serving:
Calories: 338|
Fat: 15g|
Carbs: 27g|
Fiber: 2.1g|
Protein: 23g

Sprinkle the pork chops with salt and black pepper generously.
In a high-power blender, add half of peach and pulse until a puree forms.
Reserve remaining peach.
In a wok, heat oil over medium heat and sauté shallots for about 1-2 minutes.
Add garlic and ginger and sauté for about 1 minute.
Add in remaining ingredients and bring to a boil.
Now adjust the heat to medium-low and simmer for about 4-5 minutes or until a sticky glaze forms.
Remove from heat and reserve 1/3 of the glaze and set aside.
Coat the chops with remaining glaze.
Heat a non-stick wok over medium-high heat and sear the chops for about 4 minutes from both sides.
Transfer the chops onto a plate and coat with the remaining glaze evenly.
Top with reserved chopped peach and serve.

Lamb & Spinach Bake

Prep Time: 15 mins.| Cook Time: 2 hrs. 55 mins.| Serves: 8

2 tbsp. coconut oil
2 lb. lamb necks, trimmed and cut into 2-inch pieces crosswise
Salt, as required
2 medium onions, chopped
3 tbsp. fresh ginger root, minced
4 garlic cloves, minced
2 tbsp. ground coriander
1 tbsp. ground cumin
1 tsp. ground turmeric
¼ C. unsweetened coconut milk
½ C. tomatoes, chopped
2 C. boiling water
30 oz. frozen spinach, thawed and squeezed
1½ tbsp. garam masala powder
1 tbsp. fresh lemon juice
Ground black pepper, as required

Preheat your oven to 300 ºF.
In a large-sized Dutch oven, melt coconut oil over medium-high heat and stir fry the lamb pieces with salt for about 4-5 minutes or until browned completely.
Transfer the lamb onto a plate.
Now adjust the heat to medium.
In the same pan, add onion over medium heat and sauté for about 10 minutes.
Add ginger, garlic and spices and sauté for about 1 minute.
Add in coconut milk and tomatoes and cook for about 3-4 minutes.
With an immersion blender, blend the mixture until smooth.
Add lamb, boiling water and salt and cook until boiling
Cover the pan and transfer into the oven.
Bake for approximately 2½ hours.
Now, remove the pan from oven and place over medium heat.
Stir in spinach and garam masala and cook for about 3-5 minutes.
Stir in lemon juice, salt and black pepper and remove from heat.
Serve hot.

Per Serving:
Calories: 309| Fat: 14.3g|
Carbs: 9.8g|
Fiber: 3.7g|
Protein: 35.9g

Ground Lamb With Green Peas

Prep Time: 15 mins.| Cook Time: 45 mins.| Serves: 5

1 tbsp. coconut oil
3 dried red chilies
1 (2-inch) cinnamon stick
3 green cardamom pods
½ tsp. cumin seeds
1 medium red onion, chopped
1 (¾-inch) piece fresh ginger root, minced
4 garlic cloves, minced
½ tsp. garam masala powder
½ tsp. ground coriander
½ tsp. ground cumin
½ tsp. ground turmeric
2 bay leaves
1 lb. grass-fed lean ground lamb
½ C. tomato, chopped
1½ C. water
½ C. fresh green peas, shelled
2 tbsp. plain Greek yogurt, whipped
¼ C. fresh cilantro, chopped
Salt and ground black pepper, as required

In a large-sized Dutch oven, heat oil over medium-high heat and sauté the onion for about 3-4 minutes.
Add ginger, garlic, ground spices and bay leaves and sauté for about 1 minute.
Stir in lamb and cook for about 5 minutes.
Stir in tomato and cook for about 10 minutes, stirring occasionally.
Stir in water and green peas and bring to a gentle simmer.
Adjust the heat to low and cook, covered for about 25-30 minutes.
Stir in yogurt, cilantro, salt and black pepper and cook for about 4-5 minutes
Serve hot.

Per Serving:
Calories: 226| Fat: 9.7g| Carbs: 6.4g| Fiber: 1.6g| Protein: 27.2g

ANTI-INFLAMMATORY DIET cookbook FOR BEGINNERS

SNACKS RECIPES

Green Deviled Eggs

Prep Time: 10 mins.| Serves: 6

6 hard-boiled large organic eggs
1 medium avocado, peeled, pitted and chopped
2 tsp. fresh lime juice
Salt, as required

Peel the eggs and with a knife, slice them in half vertically.
Carefully scoop out the yolks from each egg half.
In a bowl, add half of egg yolks, avocado, lime juice and salt and with a fork, mash until well combined.
Scoop the avocado mixture in the egg halves evenly and serve.

Per Serving:
Calories: 120| Fat: 9.6g| Carbs: 2.4g| Fiber: 1.6g| Protein: 6.7g

---

Spicy Pumpkin Seeds

Prep Time: 10 mins.| Cook Time: 20 mins.| Serves: 4

Per Serving:
Calories: 276| Fat: 26.1g|
Carbs: 6.4g| Fiber: 1.5g|
Protein: 8.6g

1 C. pumpkin seeds, washed and dried
2 tsp. garam masala powder
1/3 tsp. red chili powder
¼ tsp. ground cumin
¼ tsp. ground turmeric
Salt, as required
3 tbsp. coconut oil, meted
½ tbsp. fresh lemon juice

Preheat your oven to 350 ºF.
Add all ingredients except for lemon juice into a bowl and toss to coat well.
Transfer the seeds mixture onto a baking sheet.
Roast for approximately 20 minutes, flipping occasionally.
Remove from oven and set aside to cool completely before serving.
Drizzle with lemon juice and serve.

ANTI-INFLAMMATORY DIET cookbook FOR BEGINNERS

Spiced Popcorn

Prep Time: 10 mins.| Cook Time: 2 mins.| Serves: 2

3 tbsp. coconut oil
½ C. popping corn
1 tbsp. olive oil
1 tsp. ground turmeric
¼ tsp. ground cumin
¼ tsp. garlic powder
Salt, as required

In a pan, melt coconut oil over medium-high heat.
Add popping corn and cover the pan tightly.
Cook for about 1-2 minutes or until corn kernels starts to pop, shaking the pan occasionally.
Remove the pan of popcorn from heat and transfer into a large-sized heatproof bowl.
Add olive oil and spices and mix well.
Serve immediately.

Per Serving:
Calories: 331|
Fat: 28.5g| Carbs: 19g| Fiber: 4.3g|
Protein: 2.7g

Beet Chips

Prep Time: 10 mins.| Cook Time: 30 mins.| Serves: 2

1 beetroot, trimmed, peeled and thinly sliced
1 tsp. garlic, minced
1 tbsp. nutritional yeast
½ tsp. red chili powder
2 tsp. coconut oil, melted

Preheat your oven to 350 °F.
Line a baking sheet with parchment paper.
In a bowl, add beet slices and oil and toss to coat well.
Arrange the beet slices onto the prepared baking sheet in a single layer.
Bake for approximately 20-30 minutes.
Serve immediately.

Per Serving:
Calories: 52| Fat: 3.6g| Carbs: 5g| Fiber: 1g| Protein: 0.8g

Seeds Crackers

Prep Time: 15 mins.| Cook Time: 15 mins.| Serves: 6

3 tbsp. water
1 tbsp. chia seeds
3 tbsp. sunflower seeds
1 tbsp. quinoa flour
1 tsp. ground turmeric
Pinch of ground cinnamon
Salt, as required

Preheat your oven to 345 ºF.
Line a baking sheet with parchment paper.
In a bowl, add the water and chia seeds and soak them for about 15 minutes.
After 15 minutes in the bowl of chia seed mixture, add the remaining ingredients and mix well.
Spread the mixture onto the prepared baking sheet.
With a pizza cutter, cut the formed mixture into desired shapes.
Bake for approximately 20 minutes.
Remove the baking sheet of crackers from oven and place it onto a wire rack to cool completely before serving.

Per Serving:
Calories: 26| Fat: 1.6g| Carbs: 2.5g| Fiber: 1.3g|
Protein: 1g

Apple Cookies

Prep Time: 15 mins.| Cook Time: 17 mins.| Serves: 8

1/3 C. unsweetened applesauce
1/2 C. peanut butter
¼ C. gluten-free old-fashioned oats
1 tbsp. ground cinnamon
2 tbsp. ground flaxseed
2 tsp. organic vanilla extract
1 tsp. baking powder
¼ tsp. salt
1 medium apple, peeled, cored and chopped

Per Serving:
Calories: 202|
Fat: 10.5g|
Carbs: 3.3g|
Fiber: 1.8g|
Protein: 24.2g

Preheat your oven to 350 °F.
Grease a cookie sheet with cooking spray.
In a food processor, add chickpeas and remaining ingredients except for apple and pulse for a very smooth.
Transfer the mixture into a bowl.
Gently fold in the chopped apple.
With a spoon, place the mixture onto the prepared cookie sheet in a single layer and with your finger, flatten each cookie slightly.
Bake for approximately 15-17 minutes or until golden brown.
Remove the cookie sheet from oven and place onto a wire rack to cool for about 5 minutes.
Carefully remove the cookies from cookie sheet and place onto the wire rack to cool before serving.

ANTI-INFLAMMATORY DIET cookbook FOR BEGINNERS

Chicken Fingers

Prep Time: 15 mins.| Cook Time: 18 mins.| Serves: 5

Per Serving:
Calories:
202| Fat:
10.5g| Carbs:
3.3g| Fiber:
1.8g| Protein:
24.2g

Olive oil cooking spray
1 (15-oz.) can chickpeas, rinsed and drained
8 large Medjool dates, pitted

2/3 C. almond meal
½ tsp. ground turmeric
½ tsp. cayenne pepper
½ tsp. paprika
½ tsp. garlic powder
Salt and ground black pepper, as required
1 organic egg
1 lb. grass-fed skinless, boneless chicken breasts, cut into strips

Preheat your oven to 375 ºF.
Line a large-sized baking sheet with parchment paper.
In a shallow dish, beat the egg.
In another shallow dish, mix together almond meal and spices.
Coat each chicken strip with egg and then roll into spice mixture evenly
Arrange the chicken strips onto the prepared baking sheet in a single layer
Bake for approximately 16-18 minutes.
Serve warm.

Chocolate Date Bites

Prep Time: 10 mins.| Cook Time: 15 mins.| Serves: 2

1 C. Medjool dates, pitted
2 C. raw walnuts
6 tbsp. cacao powder
1¼ C. plus 3 tbsp. hemp seeds, divided
¼ tsp. sea salt
3 tbsp. almond butter
1 tbsp. coconut oil, melted

In a food processor, add the dates to and pulse until just ball forms.
Transfer the dates into a bowl and set aside.
In the food processor, add the walnuts and pulse until a fine meal is formed.
Add the cacao powder, 3 tbsp. of hemp seeds and salt and pulse until just blended.
Now add the dates, almond butter and coconut oil in food processor and pulse until a moist dough-like mixture is formed.
Transfer the date mixture into a bowl and refrigerate for about 10 minutes.
In a shallow bowl, place the remaining hemp seeds.
Make small equal-sized balls from the mixture.
Coat the balls with hemp seeds evenly.
. Place the date balls onto a baking paper-lined baking sheet and arrange in a single layer.
. Refrigerate the balls for about 2 hours before serving.

Per Serving:
Calories: 370| Fat: 27.2g| Carbs: 23.7g|
Fiber: 5.1g| Protein: 15g

Potato Sticks

Prep Time: 10 mins.| Cook Time: 15 mins.| Serves: 2

1 large russet potato, peeled and cut into 1/8-inch thick sticks lengthwise
10 curry leaves
¼ tsp. ground turmeric
¼ tsp. red chili powder
Salt, as required
1 tbsp. olive oil

Preheat your oven to 400 ºF.
Line 2 large-sized baking sheets with parchment paper.
In a large-sized bowl, add all ingredients and toss to coat well
Transfer the mixture into prepared baking sheets in a single layer.
Bake for approximately 10 minutes.
Serve immediately.

Per Serving:
Calories: 204| Fat: 7.3g| Carbs: 32.6g| Fiber: 4.2g| Protein: 3.8g

---

Almond Scones

Prep Time: 10 mins.| Cook Time: 20 mins.| Serves: 8

1 C. almonds
1 1/3 C. almond flour
¼ C. arrowroot flour
1 tbsp. coconut flour
1 tsp. ground turmeric
Salt and ground black pepper, as required
1 organic egg
¼ C. olive oil
3 tbsp. organic honey
1 tsp. organic vanilla extract

Preheat your oven to 350 ºF.
In a food processor, add almonds and pulse until chopped roughly
Transfer the chopped almonds in a large-sized bowl.
Add flours and spices and mix well
In another bowl, add remaining ingredients and beat until well combined
Add flour mixture into egg mixture and mix until well combined
Arrange a plastic wrap over cutting board
Place the dough over cutting board.
With your hands, pat into about 1-inch thick circle.
. Carefully cut the dough circle in 8 wedges
. Arrange the scones onto a cookie sheet in a single layer
. Bake for approximately 15-20 minutes.

Per Serving:
Calories: 283| Fat: 22.9g| Carbs: 13.8g| Fiber: 4g| Protein: 3.5g

ANTI-INFLAMMATORY DIET cookbook FOR BEGINNERS

SMOOTHIES

RECIPES

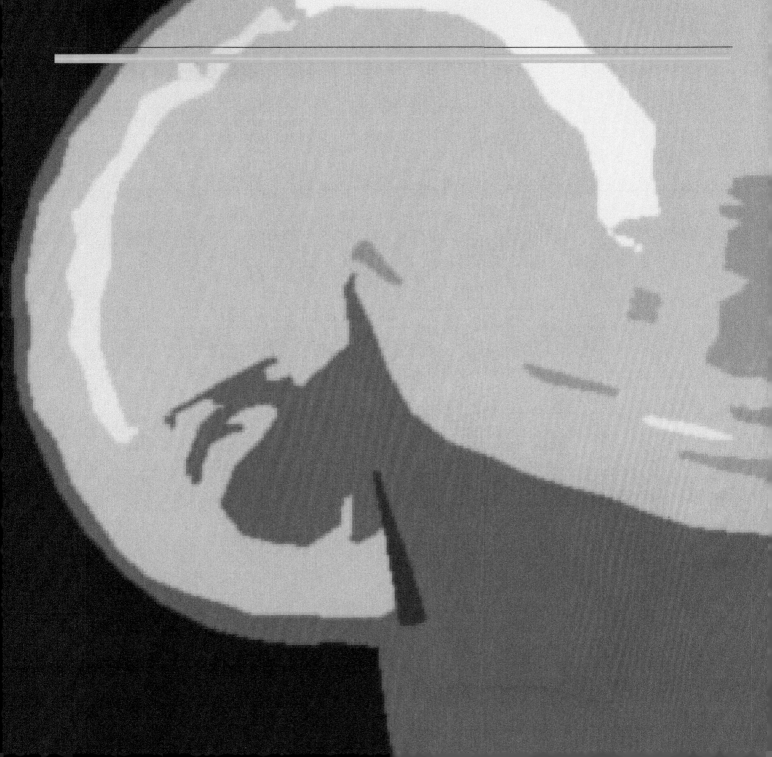

Orange Smoothie

Prep Time: 10 mins.| Serves: 2

¼ C. gluten-free rolled oats
1 orange, peeled, seeded and sectioned
1 large banana, peeled and sliced
1 C. unsweetened almond milk
½ C. ice cubes

In a high-power blender, add all the ingredients and pulse until smooth and creamy.
Transfer the smoothie into 2 serving glasses and serve immediately.

Per Serving:
Calories: 175| Fat: 3g| Carbs: 36.6g| Fiber: 5.9g| Protein: 5.9g

Peach Smoothie

Prep Time: 10 mins.| Serves: 2

1 frozen banana, peeled and chopped
1½ C. frozen peaches, pitted and chopped
½ tsp. ground ginger
½ tsp. chia seeds
1 tsp. ground turmeric
1 tsp. ground cinnamon
1 tsp. organic honey
1½ C. unsweetened almond milk

In a high-power blender, add all the ingredients and pulse until smooth and creamy.
Transfer the smoothie into 2 serving glasses and serve immediately.

Per Serving:
Calories: 148| Fat: 3.5g|
Carbs: 30.6g| Fiber: 5.1g|
Protein: 2.8g

Pear & Blueberry Smoothie

Prep Time: 10 mins.| Serves: 2

Per Serving:
Calories: 240| Fat: 8.1g| Carbs: 42.1g| Fiber: 6g| Protein: 4.8g

1 Asian pear, peeled, cored and chopped
1 C. frozen blueberries
2 Medjool dates, pitted
3 tbsp. raw cashews
1 tbsp. hemp seeds
1¼ C. water

In a high-power blender, add all the ingredients and pulse until smooth and creamy.
Transfer the smoothie into 2 serving glasses and serve immediately.

Mango & Pineapple Smoothie

Prep Time: 10 mins.| Serves: 2

1¼ C. mango, peeled, pitted and chopped
1 C. pineapple, peeled and chopped
1 tbsp. chia seeds
1 tsp. ground turmeric
½ tsp. ground ginger
½ tsp. ground cinnamon
Pinch of vanilla powder
1 tsp. coconut oil
1 C. unsweetened coconut milk
½ C. ice cubes

In a high-power blender, add all the ingredients and pulse until smooth and creamy.
Transfer the smoothie into 2 serving glasses and serve immediately.

Per Serving:
Calories: 166| Fat: 6.2g| Carbs: 30.3g| Fiber: 5.2g| Protein: 2.2g

Pineapple & Carrot Smoothie

Prep Time: 10 mins.| Serves: 2

1 C. frozen pineapple
1 large ripe banana, peeled and slice
½ tbsp. fresh ginger, peeled and chopped
¼ tsp. ground turmeric
1 C. unsweetened almond milk
½ C. fresh carrot juice
1 tbsp. fresh lemon juice

In a high-power blender, add all the ingredients and pulse until smooth and creamy.
Transfer the smoothie into 2 serving glasses and serve immediately.

Per Serving:
Calories: 139| Fat: 10.5g|
Carbs: 34.6g| Fiber: 5.4g|
Protein: 2.1g

Sweet Potato Smoothie

Prep Time: 10 mins.| Serves: 2

1 medium frozen banana, peeled and sliced
1 C. sweet potato puree
1 tsp. fresh ginger root, chopped
½ tbsp. flaxseed meal
1 tbsp. almond butter
¼ tsp. ground turmeric
¼ tsp. ground cinnamon
1 C. unsweetened almond milk
¼ C. fresh orange juice
¼ C. ice cubes

In a high-power blender, add all the ingredients and pulse until smooth and creamy.
Transfer the smoothie into 2 serving glasses and serve immediately.

Per Serving:
Calories: 242| Fat: 7.5g| Carbs: 41.7g| Fiber: 7.1g| Protein: 5.7g

ANTI-INFLAMMATORY DIET cookbook FOR BEGINNERS

Avocado & Kale Smoothie

Prep Time: 10 mins.| Serves: 2

Per Serving:
Calories: 167| Fat:
13.6g| Carbs:
11.2g| Fiber:
5.55g| Protein:
3.5g

2 C. fresh kale, tough ribs removed and chopped
2 celery stalks, chopped
½ of avocado, peeled, pitted and chopped
1 (½-inch) piece fresh ginger root, chopped
1 (½-inch) piece fresh turmeric root, chopped
1½ C. unsweetened coconut milk
¼ C. ice cubes

In a high-power blender, add all the ingredients and pulse until smooth and creamy.
Transfer the smoothie into 2 serving glasses and serve immediately.

Cucumber & Lettuce Smoothie

Prep Time: 10 mins.| Serves: 2

1 cucumber, peeled and chopped
1 C. lettuce leaves
½ C. fresh mint leaves
1 tbsp. fresh ginger root, grated
2 C. coconut water
1 tbsp. fresh lime juice
¼ C. ice cubes

In a high-power blender, add all the ingredients and pulse until smooth and creamy.
Transfer the smoothie into 2 serving glasses and serve immediately

Per Serving:
Calories: 92| Fat: 1g| Carbs: 19.1g| Fiber: 5.6g| Protein: 3.8g

Green Fruit & Veggie Smoothie

Prep Time: 10 mins.| Serves: 2

1 C. cucumber, peeled and chopped
1 pear, peeled, cored and chopped
1 green apple, cored and chopped
1 small avocado, peeled, pitted and chopped
½ tbsp. fresh dill
1 C. fresh spinach, chopped
1 celery stalk, chopped
¼ tsp. ground turmeric
1 piece fresh ginger root, peeled
1 tbsp. fresh lime juice
2 C. water

In a high-power blender, add all the ingredients and pulse until smooth and creamy.
Transfer the smoothie into 2 serving glasses and serve immediately.

Per Serving:
Calories: 319|
Fat: 20.1g|
Carbs: 38g|
Fiber: 12.5g|
Protein: 3.5g

Matcha Green Smoothie

Prep Time: 10 mins.| Serves: 2

½ C. frozen pineapple
1 C. fresh baby spinach
½ of avocado, peeled, pitted and chopped
2 tbsp. organic honey
1 tbsp. coconut oil
1 tsp. matcha green tea powder
½ C. fresh orange juice
1 C. unsweetened almond milk

In a high-power blender, add all the ingredients and pulse until smooth and creamy.
Transfer the smoothie into 2 serving glasses and serve immediately.

Per Serving:
Calories: 222|
Fat: 14.3g| Carbs:
24.5g| Fiber:
3.5g| Protein:
2.1g

ANTI-INFLAMMATORY DIET cookbook FOR BEGINNERS

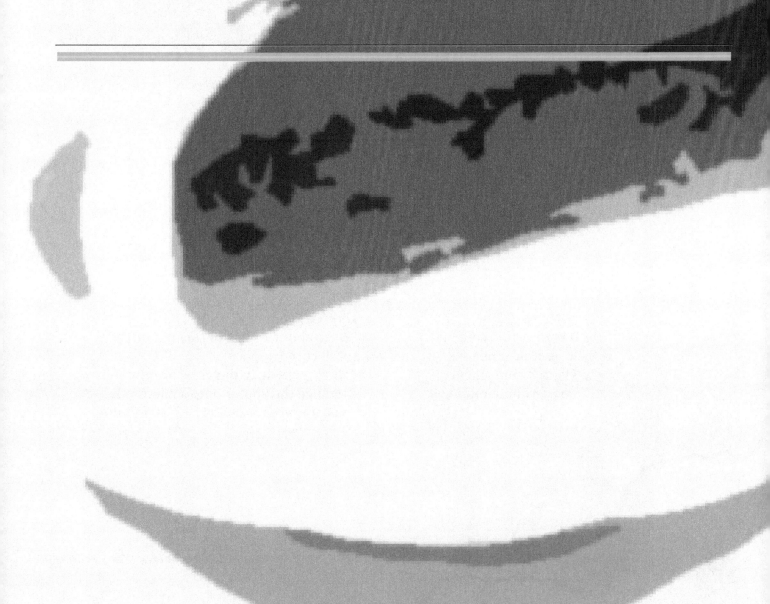

DESSERTS

RECIPES

Cinnamon Peaches

Prep Time: 10 mins.| Cook Time: 10 mins.| Serves: 4

Olive oil cooking spray
2 large peaches, halved and pitted
1/8 tsp. ground cinnamon

Preheat the grill to medium-high heat.
Grease the grill grate with cooking spray.
Arrange the peach halves on the prepared grill, cut side down.
Grill for 3-5 minutes per side.
Sprinkle with cinnamon and serve.

Per Serving:
Calories: 30| Fat: 0.2g| Carbs: 7.1g| Fiber: 1.2g| Protein: 0.7g

Spiced Apples

Prep Time: 10 mins.| Cook Time: 18 mins.| Serves: 4

4 apples, cored
¼ C. coconut oil, softened
2 tsp. ground cinnamon
1/8 tsp. ground ginger
1/8 tsp. ground nutmeg

Preheat your oven to 350 ºF.
Place about 1 tbsp. of coconut oil into each cored apple.
Then sprinkle with spices evenly.
Arrange the apples onto a baking sheet.
Bake for approximately 12-18 minutes.
Serve warm.

Per Serving:
Calories: 240| Fat: 14.1g| Carbs: 32.7g| Fiber: 6.6g| Protein: 0.7g

ANTI-INFLAMMATORY DIET cookbook FOR BEGINNERS

Berries Granita

½ C. fresh strawberries, hulled and sliced
½ C. fresh raspberries
½ C. fresh blueberries
½ C. fresh blackberries
1 tbsp. maple syrup
1 tbsp. fresh lemon juice
1 C. ice cubes, crushed

In a high-power blender, add the berries, maple syrup, lemon juice, and ice cubes and pulse on high speed until smooth.
Transfer the berry mixture into an 8x8-inch baking dish, spread evenly, and freeze for at least 30 minutes.
Remove the baking dish of granita from freezer and, with a fork, stir the granita completely.
Freeze for 2-3 hours, stirring after every 30 minutes with a fork.

Per Serving:
Calories: 46| Fat: 0.3g| Carbs: 11g| Fiber: 2.8g| Protein: 0.7g

Pumpkin Ice Cream

Prep Time: 15 mins.| Serves: 6

1 (15-oz.) can sugar-free pumpkin puree
½ C. dates, pitted and chopped
2 (14-oz.) cans unsweetened coconut milk
½ tsp. vanilla extract
1½ tsp. pumpkin pie spice
½ tsp. ground cinnamon
Pinch of salt

In a high-power blender, add all ingredients and pulse until smooth.
Transfer into an airtight container and freeze for about 1-2 hours
Now, transfer into an ice-cream maker and process according to manufacturer's directions
Return the ice-cream into the airtight container and freeze for about 1-2 hours before serving.

Per Serving:
Calories: 94| Fat: 2.2g| Carbs: 17.9g| Fiber: 4g| Protein: 1.7g

Avocado Pudding

Prep Time: 15 mins.| Serves: 4

2 C. bananas, peeled and chopped
2 ripe avocados, peeled, pitted and chopped
1 tsp. fresh lime zest, finely grated
1 tsp. fresh lemon zest, finely grated
½ C. fresh lime juice
½ C. fresh lemon juice
1/3 C. organic honey
¼ C. walnuts, chopped

Add all pudding ingredients in a high-power blender and pulse until smooth.
Divide the mousse into 4 serving glasses and refrigerate to chill for about 3 hours before serving.
Garnish with walnuts and serve.

Per Serving:
Calories: 330|
Fat: 16.2g| Carbs:
47.5g| Fiber:
6.5g| Protein: 4.g

Strawberry Souffle

Prep Time: 10 mins.| Cook Time: 15 mins.| Serves: 6

18 oz. fresh strawberries, hulled
1/3 C. organic honey, divided
5 organic egg whites, divided
4 tsp. fresh lemon juice

Preheat your oven to 350 ºF.
In a blender, ad strawberries and pulse until a puree forms.
Through a strainer, strain the seeds.
In a bowl, add strawberry puree, 3 tbsp. of honey, 2 egg whites and lemon juice and pulse until frothy and light.
In another bowl, add remaining egg whites and beat until frothy.
While beating gradually, add remaining honey and beat until stiff peaks form.
Gently, fold the egg whites into strawberry mixture.
Transfer the mixture into 6 large ramekins evenly.
Arrange the ramekins onto a baking sheet.
. Bake for approximately 10-12 minutes.
. Remove the ramekins from oven and serve immediately.

Per Serving:
Calories: 100| Fat:
0.3g| Carbs: 22.3g|
Fiber: 1.8g| Protein:
3.7g

ANTI-INFLAMMATORY DIET cookbook FOR BEGINNERS

Pineapple Upside-Down Cake

Prep Time: 15 mins.| Cook Time: 50 mins.| Serves: 6

Per Serving:
Calories: 258| Fat: 17.1g| Carbs: 21.6g|
Fiber: 2.4g| Protein: 6.1g

5 tbsp. organic honey, divided
2 (½-inch thick) fresh pineapple slices
15 fresh sweet cherries
1 C. almond flour
½ tsp. baking powder
2 organic eggs
3 tbsp. coconut oil, melted
1 tsp. organic vanilla extract

Preheat your oven to 350 ºF.

In an 8-inch round cake pan, place about 1½ tbsp. of honey evenly.

Arrange the pineapple slices and 15 cherries over honey in your desired pattern.

Bake for approximately 15 minutes.

1n a bowl, blend together almond flour and baking powder.

In another bowl, add eggs and remaining honey and beat until creamy.

In the bowl of egg mixture, add coconut oil and vanilla extract and beat until well blended.

Add flour mixture into egg mixture and mix until well blended.

Remove the cake pan from oven.

. Place the flour mixture over pineapple and cherries evenly.

. Bake for approximately 35 minutes.

. Remove the pan of cake from oven and set aside to cool for about 10 minutes.

. Carefully remove the cake from pan and place onto a serving plate.

. Cut into desired-sized slices and serve

Cherry Cobbler

Prep Time: 10 mins.| Cook Time: 25 mins.| Serves: 4

2 C. fresh cherries, pitted
¼ C. plus 1 tbsp. coconut sugar, divided
¼ C. pecans, chopped
¼ C. unsweetened coconut, shredded
¼ C. coconut flour
1 tbsp. arrowroot flour
½ tsp. ground cinnamon
Pinch of salt

Preheat your oven to 375 ºF.
In a 7x5-inch baking dish, place the cherries.
Place ¼ C. of coconut sugar over cherries evenly.
In a bowl, add 1 tbsp. of coconut sugar and remaining ingredients and mix well.
Spread pecan mixture over cherries evenly.
Bake for approximately 20-25 minutes.
Remove the baking dish of cobbler from oven and set aside to cool slightly.
Serve warm.

Per Serving: Calories: 173| Fat: 7.4g| Carbs: 27.2g| Fiber: 5.9g| Protein: 3g

Pumpkin Pie

Prep Time: 15 mins.| Cook Time: 1 hr. 5 mins.| Serves: 8

For Crust
2½ C. walnuts
1 tsp. baking soda
Salt, as required
2 tbsp. coconut oil, melted

For Filling
1 (15-oz.) can sugar-free pumpkin puree
1 tbsp. arrowroot powder
½ tsp. ground nutmeg
½ tsp. ground cinnamon
¼ tsp. ground ginger
¼ tsp. ground cardamom
¼ tsp. ground cloves
Pinch of salt
1 C. unsweetened coconut milk
3 eggs, beaten
3 tbsp. organic honey

Preheat your oven to 350 ºF.
For crust: in a food processor, add walnuts, baking soda and salt and pulse until finely ground.
Now add the coconut oil and pulse until well blended.
Place the crust mixture into a 9-inch pie dish.
With the back of a spatula, smooth the surface of crust.
Arrange the pie dish in a baking sheet.
Bake for approximately 15 minutes.
Meanwhile, for filling: in a large-sized bowl, add all ingredients and mix until well blended.
Remove the crust from oven.
. Place the mixture into crust. (Try not to overfill the crust)
. Bake for approximately 50 minutes.
. Remove the pie dish from oven and place onto the wire rack to cool for about 10 minutes.
. Freeze for about 3-4 hours before serving.

Nutritional Information per Serving:
Calories: 218| Fat: 1g| Carbs: 14.7g| Fiber: 2.9g| Protein: 5.3g

ANTI-INFLAMMATORY DIET cookbook FOR BEGINNERS

Pineapple & Mango Crisp

Prep Time: 15 mins.| Cook Time: 15 mins.| Serves: 8

For Filling
2 tbsp. coconut oil
2 tbsp. coconut sugar
1 large mango, peeled, pitted and chopped
3-4 C. fresh pineapple, peeled and cut into chunks
1/8 tsp. ground cinnamon
1/8 tsp. ground ginger

For Topping
¾ C. almonds
1/3 C. coconut, shredded
½ tsp. ground allspice
½ tsp. ground cinnamon
½ tsp. ground ginger

Per Serving:
Calories: 162| Fat: 9.2g| Carbs: 21g| Fiber: 3g| Protein: 2.7g

Preheat your oven to 375 ºF.
For filling in a pan, melt coconut oil over medium-low heat and cook coconut sugar for about 1-2 minutes, stirring continuously.
Stir in remaining ingredients and cook for about 5 minutes.
Remove the pan of filling from heat and transfer the mixture into a baking dish.
Meanwhile, for topping in a food processor, add all ingredients and pulse until a coarse meal forms.
Place the topping over filling evenly.
Bake for approximately 13-15 minutes or until top becomes golden brown.
Remove the baking dish of crisp from oven and set aside to cool slightly.
Serve warm.

BONUS

Dear reader, if you're reading this sentence, you probably haven't carefully read the description of this book on the Amazon page, where the link to buy the COLOR version is clearly indicated at the end.

But don't worry, I have a surprise for you:

SCAN THE QR CODE TO DOWNLOAD AND ENJOY THE COLOR VERSION!

SCAN ME

FREE DOWNLOAD

IBD FOOD JOURNAL

6 WEEKS MEAL PLAN

Week 1	Breakfast	Lunch	Dinner	Total Calories
Day 1	Peach Smoothie Calories: 148	Three Veggies Medley Calories: 189	Chicken & Spinach Stew Calories: 279	616
Day 2	Spiced Oatmeal Calories: 129	Shrimp in Lemon Sauce Calories: 268	Mixed Grains Chili Calories: 351	738
Day 3	Raspberry Smoothie Bowl Calories: 258	Pumpkin curry Calories: 263	Meatballs Curry Calories: 234	755
Day 4	Turmeric Bread Calories: 145	Mixed Fruit Salad Calories: 161	Chickpeas & Veggie Curry Calories: 335	641
Day 5	Spinach & Egg Scramble Calories: 257	Egg Drop Soup Calories: 64	Fruity Shrimp Curry Calories: 311	632
Day 6	Pear & Blueberry Smoothie Calories: 240	Spinach, Mushrooms & Tomato Combo Calories: 179	Pork with Pineapple Calories: 282	701
Day 7	Veggie Frittata Calories: 191	Stuffed Bell Peppers Calories: 296	Salmon in Yogurt Sauce Calories: 270	757
Week 2	Breakfast	Lunch	Dinner	Total Calories
Day 1	Fruity Chai Bowl Calories: 183	Quinoa with Asparagus Calories: 258	Beans & Lentils Soup Calories: 285	726
Day 2	Turmeric Bread Calories: 145	Beans & Mango Salad Calories: 291	Glazed Flank Steak Calories: 385	821
Day 3	Blueberry Muffins Calories: 252	Veggie Kabobs Calories: 181	Sea Bass with Veggies Calories: 280	713
Day 4	Matcha Green Smoothie Calories: 222	Mushroom Soup Calories: 56	Shrimp & Veggies Curry Calories: 311	589
Day 5	Spinach & Egg Scramble Calories: 257	Zucchini Lettuce Wraps Calories: 60	Spicy Lamb Curry Calories: 319	636
Day 6	Quinoa & Pumpkin Porridge	Halibut Kabobs Calories: 235	Lentil & Quinoa Stew	812

		Calories: 285		Calories: 292	
Day 7	Veggie Frittata Calories: 191	Prawns with Asparagus Calories: 231	Meatballs Curry Calories: 234		656
Week 3	**Breakfast**	**Lunch**	**Dinner**	**Total Calories**
Day 1	Orange Smoothie Calories: 175	Three Veggies Medley Calories: 189	Snapper Parcel Calories: 390	754
Day 2	Banana Pancakes Calories: 145:	Citrus Greens Salad Calories: 256	Chicken & Spinach Stew Calories: 279	680
Day 3	Apple Omelet Calories: 284	Prawns with Asparagus Calories: 231	Spicy Kidney Beans Curry Calories: 221	736
Day 4	Avocado & Kale Smoothie Calories: 167	Greens & Seeds Salad Calories: 184	Turkey & Chickpeas Chili Calories: 301	652
Day 5	Blueberry Muffins Calories: 252	Quinoa with Asparagus Calories: 258	Beef & Mushroom Soup Calories: 222	732
Day 6	Spinach & Egg Scramble Calories: 257	Chicken Salad Calories: 300	Beans & Veggie Soup Calories: 289	846
Day 7	Fruity Chai Bowl Calories: 183	Scallops in Yogurt Sauce Calories: 191	Mixed Grains Chili Calories: 351	725
Week 4	**Breakfast**	**Lunch**	**Dinner**	**Total Calories**
Day 1	Raspberry Smoothie Bowl Calories: 258	Three Veggies Medley Calories: 189	Poached Salmon Calories: 259	706
Day 2	Turmeric Bread Calories: 145	Spiced Ground Beef Calories: 352	Chickpeas & Veggie Curry Calories: 335	832
Day 3	Spiced Oatmeal Calories: 129	Stuffed Zucchini Calories: 169	Pork Chops with Peach Calories: 338	636
Day 4	Spinach & Egg Scramble Calories: 257	Citrus Greens Salad Calories: 256	Snapper Parcel Calories: 390	903
Day 5	Peach Smoothie Calories: 148	Scallops in Yogurt Sauce Calories: 191	Spicy Kidney Beans Curry Calories: 221	560
Day 6	Fruity Chai Bowl Calories: 183	Greens & Seeds Salad Calories: 184	Spicy Lamb Curry Calories: 319	686
Day 7	Quinoa & Pumpkin Porridge Calories: 285	Veggie Kabobs Calories: 181	Chicken & Spinach Stew Calories: 279	745
Week 5	**Breakfast**	**Lunch**	**Dinner**	**Total Calories**

	Breakfast	Lunch	Dinner	Total Calories
Day 1	Quinoa & Pumpkin Porridge Calories: 285	Egg Drop Soup Calories: 64	Pork Chops with Peach Calories: 338	687
Day 2	Avocado & Kale Smoothie Calories: 167	Duck with Bok Choy Calories:317	Three Beans Chili Calories: 342	826
Day 3	Banana Pancakes Calories: 145	Spiced Ground Beef Calories: 352	Spicy Kidney Beans Curry Calories: 221	718
Day 4	Spiced Oatmeal Calories: 129	Potato & Corn Curry Calories: 135	Walnut Crusted Salmon Calories: 350	614
Day 5	Apple Omelet Calories: 284	Greens & Seeds Salad Calories: 184	Turkey & Chickpeas Chili Calories: 301	769
Day 6	Cucumber & Lettuce Smoothie Calories: 92	Chicken Salad Calories: 300	Mixed Grains Chili Calories: 351	743
Day 7	Fruity Chai Bowl Calories: 183	Quinoa with Asparagus Calories: 258	Snapper Parcel Calories: 390	831
Week 6	**Breakfast**	**Lunch**	**Dinner**	**Total Calories**
Day 1	Orange Smoothie Calories: 175	Prawns with Asparagus Calories: 231	Mixed Veggies Curry Calories: 352	758
Day 2	Turmeric Bread Calories: 145	Citrus Greens Salad Calories: 256	Turkey & Chickpeas Chili Calories: 301	702
Day 3	Banana Pancakes Calories: 145	Scallops in Yogurt Sauce Calories: 191	Chickpeas & Veggie Curry Calories: 335	671
Day 4	Apple Omelet Calories: 284	Stuffed Zucchini Calories: 169	Beef & Mushroom Soup Calories: 222	675
Day 5	Mango & Pineapple Smoothie Calories: 166	Potato & Corn Curry Calories: 135	Spiced Whole Chicken Calories: 514	815
Day 6	Blueberry Muffins Calories: 252	Three Veggies Medley Calories: 189	Poached Salmon Calories: 259	700
Day 7	Raspberry Smoothie Bowl Calories: 258	Scallops in Yogurt Sauce Calories: 191	Beans & Veggie Soup Calories: 289	738

SHOPPING LIST

Poultry, Meat & Seafood

whole chicken
chicken breasts
chicken thighs
lean ground turkey
cooked duck
sirloin steak
flank steak
cooked beef meat
lean ground beef
pork tenderloin
pork chops
boneless lamb
lamab necks
lean ground lamb
salmon
halibut
cod
tilapia
sea bass
snapper
shrimp
prawns
scallops

Dairy:

eggs
yogurt

Vegetables & Fresh Herbs:

spinach
kale
bok choy
arugula

collard greens
mushrooms
bell pepper
pumpkin
eggplant
broccoli
broccolini
asparagus
green peas
tomato
cucumber
carrot
potato
sweet potato
zucchini
cauliflower
corn
celery
Brussels sprout
cabbage
lettuce
salad greens
onion
shallot
scallion
lemongrass
chives
garlic
ginger
turmeric root
jalapeño pepper
Serrano pepper
chipotle pepper
red chili pepper
green chili pepper
lemon
lime

ANTI-INFLAMMATORY DIET cookbook FOR BEGINNERS

curry leaves
basil
mint
rosemary
thyme
parsley
cilantro
dill
oregano

Fruit

strawberries
raspberries
blueberries
blackberries
cranberries
cherries
mango
apple
pear
peach
pineapple
orange
grapefruit
banana
dates
avocado

Grains, Nuts & Seeds

oats
quinoa
bulgur
barley
brown rice
black beans
red kidney beans
white beans
cannellini beans
chickpeas
lentils
almonds
pecans
walnuts

cashews
chia seeds
sesame seeds
hemp seeds
flaxseeds
flaxseed meal

Seasoning & Dried Herbs

salt
black pepper
white pepper
cayenne pepper
paprika
red chili powder
red pepper flakes
garlic powder
cinnamon
ginger
nutmeg
cardamom
turmeric
cumin
coriander
sumac
bay leaves
curry paste
curry powder
garam masala powder
thyme
oregano

Extra:

almond milk
coconut milk
olive oil
coconut oil
sesame oil
MCT oil
Olive oil cooking spray
almond meal
almond flour
coconut flour
chickpea flour

arrowroot flour
arrowroot powder
arrowroot starch
baking powder
baking soda
protein powder
matcha green tea powder
cacao powder
Dijon mustard
nutritional yeast
apple cider vinegar
vanilla extract
coconut aminos
fish sauce
coconut sugar
stevia
organic honey
maple syrup
almond butter
sugar-free pumpkin puree
unsweetened dried cranberries
unsweetened coconut
chicken broth
beef broth
vegetable broth

ANTI-INFLAMMATORY DIET cookbook FOR BEGINNERS

CONCLUSION

The anti-inflammatory cookbook is a great resource for people looking to improve their health by reducing inflammation. The recipes are easy to follow, and the ingredients are readily available. I highly recommend this cookbook to anyone interested in improving their health.

INDEX

ANTI-INFLAMMATORY DIET cookbook FOR BEGINNERS

ANTI-INFLAMMATORY DIET cookbook FOR BEGINNERS